THE THIRTY-TWO VIDYAS

K. NARAYANASWAMI AIYAR

GYAN

Published by

GYAN

Gyan Publishing House
5, Ansari Road
Daryaganj, New Delhi-110002
Phone: 011-47034999, 9811692060
E-mail: books@gyanbooks.com

Distribution Network
gyanbooks.com
India, USA, Canada, UK, Australia

ISBN: 978-93-7133-796-0 (HB)

First Published, 1916

2nd Impression 2025

Printed at: Gyan Press, Delhi.

THE THIRTY-TWO VIDYAS
Author: K. NARAYANASWAMI AIYAR

THE

THIRTY-TWO VIDYĀS

BY

K. NARAYANASWAMI AIYAR

Author of

Thirty Minor Upanishads, The Purāṇas in the Light of Modern Science, Yoga: Lower and Higher, Laghu Yoga-Vāsishtha, etc.

PUBLISHED BY THE AUTHOR
THEOSOPHICAL SOCIETY, ADYAR, MADRAS, INDIA
1916

FOREWORD

The subject of this work is rather a very difficult and abstruse one. Only those that have theoretically at least grasped the principles of the higher yoga can follow the teachings contained in it. For which purpose, the book I have recently published called *Yoga: Lower and Higher* will be greatly serviceable. When especially the higher yoga therein is grasped, it will be then easy to follow the trend of ideas herein.

The word "Vidyās" does not signify, as stated at the beginning of this book, mere knowledge but different kinds of meditations which conduce to the getting of knowledge and other results. These Vidyās are based upon the authority of the Major or 12 Upanishads amplified in the minor ones. Of them, it is the Gāyatrī-Vidyā that is the most important. It forms the key by which we are enabled to unlock the mysteries contained in the other Vidyās. And it is upon it that the Upanishads throw more light. To me, it is the one Vidyā that has been of immense benefit.

I do not think myself that I have done full justice to the subject. Nay it is not possible. Only an occult person that has his Divine Vision opened to the higher states can do justice to it. In the hope that some person here or there who is practising the lower yoga may be induced to practise the higher or that one going into the higher yoga may find herein some practical suggestions, I place this book before the public.

June 1916. K. NARAYANASWAMI AIYAR

CONTENTS

VIḌYĀS

In the Major, or the 12, Upanishaḍs as well as in the *Veḍānṭa-Sūṭras*, there occur what are called, Viḍyās. The Upanishaḍs make mention of them in different places, while in the latter, Aḍhyāya III, Pāḍa III. takes them up together and discusses them: what they are, what they tend to, and whether they should be taken up for meditation together or separately, and so on. If we go into them, we find they are different kinds of meditation. But the word Viḍyā means knowledge, coming as it does from the root *viḍ*, to know. Why should the word Viḍya, meaning knowledge, be applied to meditation? In the *Veḍānṭa-Sūṭras* III, III. 14 S'rī S'aṅkara in his commentary says thus: आध्यानपूर्वकाय सम्यग्दर्शनायेति "For the purpose of Samyag-ḍars'ana which has Ḍhyāna for its anṭecedent." Again in III, III. 59, of the same work, the great commentator says: आसां फलमुपास्यविषयसाक्षात्करणम् "The fruit of Upāsya (worshipped object) is Sākshāṭ-karaṇa" (immediate perception). In the above two quotations, two words are used on either side. We have to understand them. The first pair is Ḍhyāna and Upāsanā. Ḍhyāna is, we know, meditation. Technically it is the second of the three stages of mind-control. But the word Upāsanā is generally applied to a long continued meditation; it comes from roots: *upa*, near, and *ās*, to sit. Hence it enables one to wait upon the object of meditation. The word Upāsī is therefore applied to one who has undergone a long course of meditation and who is therefore able to be near unto his Ishta-Ḍevaṭā or other object of meditation. The other two pairs that express the results of meditation are Samyag-ḍarśana and Sākshāṭkaraṇa. Samyag-ḍarśana is literally "well-seeing," or true vision, while the latter word means face-to-faceness, or even identity, according to aḍvaiṭic aspect. Thus ordinary meditation upon any object makes the meditator to have more and more knowledge of the object meditated upon, while, in its latest phase, the final result brings about the face-to-faceness of such an object. In the first case, the knowledge comes upon us gradually and completely, but we do not know wherefrom. Then it is Paroksha or indirect. In the second case, we see directly the object, and hence Aparoksha, or direct knowledge, is obtained. As knowledge, direct and indirect, is the result of such meditations, the word Viḍyā is applied to the subject on hand.

But then do not all kinds of meditations produce knowledge? Why not call them all Viḍyās? No. It is only some kinds of meditations that are here classed under the category of Viḍyās. What they are, we shall proceed to state. In Hinḍūism, as in other religions, the one *summum bonum* of man is God. As all meditations are only means to reach God, we shall have to consider the different phases of God-manifestation, in order to understand the present question. The *Veḍānṭa-Sūṭras* take up the three broad distinctions of Nirguṇa, Saguṇa and Praṭīka (Praṭimā being included in the last), or the unconditioned, the conditioned, and images (symbolic or otherwise). As regards the first, no meditation by itself alone will enable us to reach It. Going and coming are predicable of conditioned states only. In the case of the unconditioned, we are It. Only the veils have to be removed to realise It. It being above thought, our meditation, being but mental, will not by itself enable us to reach It. As the *Veḍānṭa-Sūṭras* put it under III, III. 30: यथा लोके ग्रामप्राप्तौ देशान्तरप्रापणः पन्था अपेक्ष्यते नाऽऽरोग्यप्राप्तावेवमिहापीति । "If we want to reach some village, we have to proceed on a path leading thither: but no moving on a path is required when we wish to attain freedom from sickness." Just as a medical Doctor has to step in in order to remove the disease, so also the divine Doctor who has realised the Absolute has to step in, when the disciple is ready to remove the disease of Māyā afflicting his soul. It is only in other cases that action of any kind is required to reach the goal.

As regards image worship, the two words used in Samskṛṭ are Praṭimā and Praṭīka. The former stands for ordinary images: the latter for symbolic images. Regarding the latter, there are two Sūṭras, the 4th and the 5th in Aḍhyāya IV, Pāḍa I. of *Veḍānṭa-Sūṭras*:

न प्रतीकेन हि सः ॥ ४ ॥ ब्रह्मदृष्टिरुत्कर्षात् ॥ ५ ॥

Both when translated, according to Thibaut, with the ellipses supplied, run thus: "Not in the Symbol (is the Self to be contemplated): for he (the meditating person may) not (view symbols as being the Self)." "A contemplation of Brahman (is to be superinduced on symbols of Brahman) on account of the exaltation (thereby bestowed on symbols)." In the second of the above Sūṭras, Brahma-Ḍṛshti is translated as a contemplation on Brahman. We have not to degrade God to symbols, but to exalt symbols to God. The ideas in the *Sūṭra-Bhāshya* may be put thus: In worldly matters, if we should regard a master as a servant, we degrade him. On the contrary, we elevate the servant by applying to him the name of the master for whom he works. Similarly we have to treat the symbolic images by rising from the image to the higher. But then what is the difference between Praṭīka worship and Viḍyās? There is what is called Āḍiṭya-Viḍyā and there is also Āḍiṭya-Upāsanā. In the ordinary Āḍiṭya-Upāsanā, the devotee takes up the ordinary form of the sun that he sees through the physical eyes, and meditates upon it. But in the Āḍiṭya-Viḍyā treated of in the *Chhānḍogya-Upanishaḍ*, I, vi. 6, the meditation is on the golden Purusha within the sun, having golden whiskers, nails, etc., and being of a golden colour from head to foot. From this, it is clear that the meditation in the latter case is internal and called Ahamgraha-Upāsanā, since it is associated with Aham, or I; and that in the former it is external and called Praṭīka-Upāsanā.

Then there is another Sūṭra in the *Vedānṭa-Sūṭras* where an important hint is given to us as to the stage which those reach that are Praṭīka-worshippers. Aḍhyāya IV, Pāḍa III. Sūṭra 15 says, as commented upon, thus: प्रतीकालम्बनान्वर्जयित्वा सर्वानन्यान्विकारालम्बनान्नयति ब्रह्मलोकमिति . . . । यो हि ब्रह्मक्रतुः सब्राह्ममैश्वर्यमासीदेदिति श्लिष्यते 'तं यथा यथोपासते तदेव भवन्ति' इति श्रुतिः । न तु प्रतीकेषु ब्रह्मक्रतुत्वमस्ति प्रतीकप्रधानत्वादुपासनस्य । "Excepting those who take their stand on symbol (who meditate upon certain things as symbolically representing Brahman), *that person* (*who is not a man*) leads all others who take their stand on the Kārya or affected Brahman to the world of Brahman. . . . For he whose meditation is fixed on Brahman reaches lordship like that of Brahman according to the scriptural relation: In whatever form they meditate on Him, that they become themselves. In the case of symbols, on the other hand, meditation is not fixed on Brahman, the symbol being the chief element in meditation." Here the words that have to be noted are: "that person who is not a man". In Samskṛṭ it is the "Amānava-Purusha". It is needless to state that the words "affected Brahman" occurring in the above quotation mean the Saguṇa Brahman of effects. What do the words Amānava-Purusha mean? And where do they occur? It is a Purusha, or Being, who is not man, who is superhuman. It means that that Being does not belong to the present Mānushya or human evolution, but to a former. If we go into the context of these words, we find that this Being is a functionary appointed to conduct men from *a certain stage* to

Saguṇa Brahman. In order to understand this stage, we have to digress a little. We all have known of the two paths, Ḍevayāna and Piṭṛyāna, or the Path of Ḍevas or light, and the Path of Piṭṛs or darkness. We learn from the Upanishaḍs and the *Veḍānṭa-Sūṭras*, that both paths lead to the chanḍra or moon: the Ḍeva-path leading through the sun to the moon, and the Piṭṛ-path leading through Piṭṛ-loka to the moon. In the former path, the souls have the option of going still higher than the moon or returning to this earth, whereas in the latter the souls cannot but return to this earth, their Vāsanās not having been exhausted. When the souls of the right-hand path wish to go higher than the moon, it is stated in the *Chhānḍogya-Upanishaḍ* that they go from the moon to Viḍyuṭ (lightning), where the Amānava-purușha comes to conduct them still higher, viz. to the world of Saguṇa Brahman.

According to the Theosophical rendering, the souls after death go to Ḍevachan, which is in the Svarga or mental world. In it, there are sub-planes. The moon must therefore be in one of the sub-planes of Svarga—which is the fifth sub-plane where the Kāraṇa Sarīra is, as I have stated in my previous writings. Thus it is clear that all worship of images, whether it is symbolical or otherwise, leads a person to the Rūpa planes of Svarga, and no further. From there, the Arūpa planes of the mental world up to Saguṇa Brahman will have to be scaled through Viḍyās alone. The Viḍyās therefore begin where the Praṭīka worship ends in its results. In lieu of the Amānava-Purusha, a Jīvanmukta of a Guru may act.

NUMBER OF VIDYĀS

As regards the number of Vidyās, we find that, in his translation of S'rī Rāmānuja's commentary on the *Gīṭā*, Mr. Govindāchāriar has disclosed to us 32 Vidyās, and gives a list of them with a note of the passages in the Upanishads. Comparing them with the references to the Vidyās mentioned in his commentary by S'rī Sankara, there are two Vidyās omitted, the Udgītha and Purusha. However the list of Vidyās given therein is more exhaustive, and contains almost all the important ones. They are:

(1) Īs'vara	(17) Gāyatrī
(2) Parama-Purusha	(18) Us'asti-Kahola
(3) Sad-vidyā	(19) Antarāditya
(4) Ānandamaya	(20) Upakos'ala
(5) Paramjyoti	(21) Madhu
(6) S'āṇdilya	(22) Bālāki
(7) Paryanka	(23) Ākās'a
(8) Uddālaka	(24) Prāṇa
(9) Aksharākshara	(25) Pratardana
(10) Bhūma	(26) Nachiketa
(11) Gārgi-Akshara	(27) Vais'vānara
(12) Satyakāma	(28) Samvarga
(13) Dahara	(29) Pañchāgni
(14) Angushtha Mātrah	(30) Akshi
(15) Jotishām-Jyotih	(31) Bhṛgu-Vāruṇi
(16) Maitreyī	(32) S'rīmannyāsa beside Udgītha and Purusha.

If we go into the above list, we find that the majority of them treat of the Saguṇa Brahman in his different aspects. But there are other Viḍyās treating of the different elements, Sun, etc. As said before, the Viḍyās begin with the Kāraṇa S'arīra and go up to Saguṇa Brahman. It will be proved later on in Gāyaṭrī-Viḍyā that in the Kāraṇa S'arīra, which has its centre in the heart, there are these elements and the Sun, etc. Hence all the Viḍyās relate directly or indirectly to the worship of Saguṇa Brahman. They make us worship the lower Brahman directly or through the elements, etc., and lead us to it.

The Fruits of Viḍyās

The fruits of these Viḍyās are according to the *Veḍānṭa-Sūṭras* three in number. They are, (1) दुरितक्षय Ḍuriṭakshaya; (2) ऐश्वर्यप्राप्ति Aisvaryaprāpṭi; and (3) क्रममुक्ति Kramamukṭi. The first is the warding off of calamities or misfortunes. This is said to be the visible result. The more the Viḍyā is practised, the more the warning is given by the Guru or Ishta-Ḍevaṭā of the impending danger. Then comes the invisible result, through which a man gains the invisible Aisvaryas, viz., Siḍḍhis or occult powers, which render the possessor invincible in the outer world. The last is Kramamukṭi, or release by successive steps. This is the one where the Upāsaka becomes gifted with perfect knowledge. This occurs when he reaches Saguṇa Brahman Itself.

Then the discussion begins in the *Veḍānṭa-Sūṭras* as to whether the different Viḍyās can be cumulated and meditated upon as one or as many, and so on. For this, the reader is asked to turn to the pages of *Veḍānṭa-Sūṭras* and read Aḍhyāya III, Pāḍa III. as a whole.

Thus we find from the scriptures that, through the practice of the Viḍyās, we are able to reach the Saguṇa Brahman from the chanḍra-world, and thereby gain its omniscience or perfect knowledge. Along with it, the Upāsaka is able to be proof against all accidents and to develop Siḍḍhis, if he is so disposed. The primary object of the Viḍyās is to attain the Saguṇa Brahman at present, and eventually the Nirguṇa. The other results of Siḍḍhis, etc., may or may not be worked for by the disciple.

GĀYAṬRĪ-VIḌYĀ

INTRODUCTION

Two things have to be clearly borne in mind in the Upanishaḍic Instructions. The first is that man should not be studied as isolated from the Universe. As the Upanishaḍs put it, the Āḍhyāṭmic and the Āḍhiḍaivic, the microsmic and macrosmic aspects should both be taken into consideration by a true occult student. Should the study go on from the standpoint of the segregated unit of man alone, it will end in Black Magic, as H. P. B. put it. Hence the *Bṛhaḍāraṇyaka-* and *Chhānḍogya-Upanishaḍs*—which are the biggest of all and which, in my opinion, are veritable forests of occult knowledge—dwell on these two aspects of Aḍhyāṭma and Aḍhiḍaiva, and correlate man with the Universe.

The second point I would put to occult students and to Hinḍūs especially, is the doubt which occurs to them ever and anon in their study, as it occurred at first to me: whether the occult *Instructions* are borne out by Hinḍū literature, or lead us away from it into a wilderness. For it should be admitted that Hinḍūism has more of the occult element in it than have other religions. Therefore to the Hinḍū the query often presents itself: "Is there any trace at least, of the occult *Instructions* now given in the Hindū writings?" Even should not such a doubt present itself, as it does not to many, I would suggest that if Hindū occult students ferret out from their religious literature the authorities or passages which correspond to occult writings, they would be amply rewarded by being vouchsafed more hints on the questions before them. They will be able to work out the occult *Instructions* with more of details from the hints afforded by the Upanishaḍs. Thus practically and theoretically more of progress ensues to the student that works in this manner.

First let us take up Gāyaṭrī as a Manṭra. If we enter into the department of Manṭras in Hinḍūism, we find there are many in number that are held very sacred, and that have been made the subject of initiation by the Guru to his disciple. From time immemorial, the ceremony of initiation has been going on, so that even in this degraded age of ours, the farce has been kept up without the underlying reality. Of these Manṭras, those which are most in vogue in the outside world in India are the Manṭra under consideration, the Pañchākṣhara (five-lettered one), and the Aṣhtākṣhara (eight-lettered one). The last is the one dedicated to Vishṇu, and the middle one to Mahāḍeva. Of these three Manṭras—nay, of all—the Gāyaṭrī is reputed to be the highest. Manu in His *Smṛṭi*, (ch. II. verse 83) says:

एकाक्षरं परं ब्रह्म प्राणायामः परं तपः ।
गायत्र्यास्तु परं नास्ति मौनात्सत्यं विशिष्यते ॥

"The one-lettered Akshara (syllable) is Param-Brahma: Prāṇāyāma is the supreme Ṭapas: there is no higher (Manṭra) than Gāyaṭrī: better than taciturnity (or the vow of silence) is Saṭyam (truth)."

Again Manu says that a Ḍvija should utter Gāyaṭrī at least, whether he performs Sānḍhyā or not.

If we go throughout India, we find that it is the Gāyaṭrī Manṭra that is the universal property of all Ḍvijas, or twice-born. At the time of the sacred ceremony of Upanayana, the investiture of the holy thread, corresponding to the First Initiation leading to Ṭurīya, the three higher castes should, as a matter of course, be initiated into Gāyaṭrī; this initiation renders them Ḍvijas. Whereas they were first born into the physical body given to them by their parents, they are now born into the second or spiritual, imparted to them through the Manṭra, by the Guru. But as regards the five-lettered or eight-lettered Manṭra, it was and is optional with them to be initiated into it. Therefore it is clear from both authorities and usage, that Gāyaṭrī is the highest of all Manṭras as well as the most universal.

And why? Since it leads us to Ṭurīya, the highest of stages, whereas the other Manṭras lead us but to one or other aspect of the Hinḍū Trinity—S'iva or Vishṇu. Nowadays, people, without understanding this highest aspect of the Manṭra, degrade it, and associate it, in meditation, with a form of S'akṭi, or with Vishṇu or S'iva. Not that such a kind of meditation will have no effect; but it is not the highest form of it. There are some Ḍhyāna-S'lokas, gifting the Gāyaṭrī-Ḍevaṭā with a form clad in a white cloth and other white things, current in the lips of some of our people. Such a description is not to be found in any authoritative texts like the Upanishaḍs, but in some palmyra-leaf manuscripts only. But going into *Chhānḍogya-Upanishaḍ*, we come across Gāyaṭrī-Viḍya in Aḍhyāya III, Khaṇda XII. which is concluded in the succeeding Khaṇda or chapter. If the two chapters be carefully studied with S'rī S'aṅkara's *Commentary*, a lot of information is obtained, which gives us the clue to the greatness of the Gāyaṭrī, the Manṭra being one which should not be imparted at this stage to all who are not Aḍhikāris, or qualified for it.

Meanwhile I may refer readers to the utterances of S'rī Kṛshṇa in reply to a question of Yuḍhishthira, as recorded in the *Mahābhāraṭa*. In S'ānṭiparva Mōkshaḍharma, chapters CIX. and CX. Bhīṣhma relates the case of a Brāhmaṇa who attained the highest state through the mere uttering of Gāyaṭrī. The episode of Gāyaṭrī therein related describes how all the Higher Powers waited on the Brāhmaṇa, and how even Brahmā came forward to receive him. Thus is the principle illustrated that if Gāyaṭrī-japa (recitation) alone is followed by one without seeking the lower forms, all powers are at his feet.

GĀYAṬRĪ-VIḌYĀ

Going into Gāyaṭrī-Viḍyā itself, we shall analyse first *Chhānḍogya-Upanishaḍ*, chapter XII. of Aḍhyāya III, and then go into the next chapter. The word Gāyaṭrī is divided there into two words signifying

गायति च 'sings out' and त्रायते च 'protects'. Gāyaṭrī is thus able to protect a person through its singing or uttering. *Bṛhaḍāraṇyaka* attaches to its first syllable another meaning, viz., 'Gāyas or Prāṇas,' as is evident from V, XIV. 4. Hence it is said to protect the Prāṇas. This chapter is composed of nine Manṭras. The fifth Manṭra states सैषा चतुष्पदा षड्विधा गायत्री, viz., Gâyaṭrī has four feet and is sixfold. What are the four feet? The next Manṭra and *Bṛhaḍāraṇyaka-Upanishaḍ* (VII. xiv. 3 and 4) speak of the fourth state as Ṭurīya; from the sixth Manṭra it is evident that even these four pāḍas of Gâyaṭrī form but a quarter amsʹa, or portion, of the Immortal One, and Sʹrī Sʹankara in his *Commentary* states that Gâyaṭrī with its three feet represents the three worlds of form, while the fourth is the formless. In the above sixth Manṭra, the three-footed one is in Ḍivi, or Heaven, the third world.

What about the sixfold nature? There are two aspects, man and the universe, to be taken notice of, and in each of them three again. In Man, they are the Sʹarīra (body), the Hṛḍaya (heart in it) and the Prāṇas in the heart. Similarly in the universe there are (1) the Pṛṭhivī or universe-matter, (2) all Bhūṭas or living beings, and (3) Vāk (speech or sound vibrations which evoke the Prāṇas in man). In this, the first lesson that we have to learn is that we shall not be able to get the full force of the Gāyaṭrī unless we correlate the universe with man. It is a fact known to us all that the different bodies of man correspond to and lie in the different planes of the universe. The seat in the body where Gāyaṭrī has to be uttered is the Hṛḍaya, or heart. Its correspondence in the universe is Bhūṭas, or living beings. And just as the anāhaṭa s'abda, or sounds, arise from the Prāṇas in the heart, so is Vāk the producer of sounds in the universe. Hence in order to affect the universe from the heart, Vāk has to be utilised.

Having thus understood that there are three things in man which can be related to their counterparts in the universe, let us go into their practical application. From the above it is clear that the Gāyaṭrī-japa has to be carried on in the heart, and that the Manṭra has to be uttered therein. Let us take the Manṭra itself, and analyse it. It is composed of the words ॐ (Om), भूः (Bhūḥ), भुवः (Bhuvaḥ), सुवः (Suvaḥ), तत् (Ṭaṭ), सवितुः (Saviṭuḥ), वरेण्यं (vareṇyaṃ), भर्गः (bhargaḥ), देवस्य (Ḍevasya), धीमहि (ḍhīmahi), धियः (dhiyaḥ), यः (yaḥ), नः (naḥ), प्रचोदयात् (prachoḍayāṭ). After uttering Praṇava and the names of the three worlds (Vyāhṛṭis, as they are called), we say: "We meditate on the ineffable effulgence of that resplendent Saviṭā (Paramāṭmā or Sun); may He illuminate our Buḍḍhi (understanding)." In the above Manṭra, the two words "we" and "our" have to be noted, as laying stress on the unselfish character of the Manṭra.

As regards Manṭras in general, Manu (ch. II. verse 85) says:

विधियज्ञाज्जपयज्ञो विशिष्टो दशभिर्गुणैः ।
उपांशुः स्याच्छतभिः सहस्रो मानसः स्मृतः ॥

"Better than Viḍhiyajñas (sacrifices) is Japa ten times: one hundred times is the inaudible uttering: one thousand times is the mental."

Hence it is clear that the mental uttering of Gāyaṭrī has far more effect than the audible or inaudible. After both the latter have been gone through, there occurs the stage when it is involuntarily repeated in the heart. Hence uttering mentally the Manṭra, the disciple has to couple with it the thought underlying the words. Stationed in the heart, he has to rise, from Bhūḥ (earth) to Bhuvaḥ (astral), and then to Suvaḥ (heaven). Relating these worlds to the three bodies, he has to rise from the Sṭhūla (gross) to the Sūkshma (subtle), and then to the Kāraṇa) causal), and then meditating on the third body, or world, which is nothing but the auric egg or lotus full of effulgence, he has to transcend it to the Ṭurīya or fourth state, where the outer crust of the egg is broken, and he unifies himself with all creatures.

In order to do it, the closing Manṭras 7, 8 and 9 of chapter xiii. of Aḍhyāya III of *Chhānḍogya-Upanishaḍ* give the hint which is amplified in the next chapter. In them are mentioned three kinds of Ākāsa, the outer, the inner and the one within the (lotus of the) heart. Here we have to understand the relationship between these three kinds of Ākāsa and the three bodies. If we go into *Bṛhaḍāraṇyaka*, we find our Purusha, or human consciousness, functions in the two eyes as Inḍra and Inḍrāṇi, or Virāt, during the Jāgraṭ, or waking condition. In the Svapna, or dreaming condition, the two unite as one in the Anṭar-Hṛḍaya-Ākāsa, or the Ākāsa in the heart, but outside the Prāṇas, as will be evident later on. There is in it their food, called Loma-Piṇda, or the red lump. After being refreshed, the unified Purusha retires during Sushupṭi into the network within the heart, but inside the Prāṇas.

Bṛhaḍāraṇyaka-Upanishaḍ, IV, II. 2, 3 begins: इन्धो ह वै नामैष योऽयं दक्षिणेऽक्षन्पुरुषस्तं वा एतमिन्धꣳ सन्तमिन्द्र इत्याचक्षते परोक्षेणैव . . . ॥ अथैतद्वामेऽक्षणि पुरुषरूपमेषास्य पत्नी विराट् तयोरेष सꣳस्तावो य एषोऽन्तर्हृदय आकाशोऽथैनयोरेतदन्नं य एषोऽन्तर्हृदये लोहितपिण्डो . . . ॥ "Indra is verily the name of that Purusha who dwells in the right eye: Him whose true name is Indha, they call Indra by an indirect name .... Again that which in the shape of a Purusha dwells in the left eye is his wife, the Virāt. The union of them is the Ākāsa within the heart: again their food is the red lump within the heart."

The same Upanishaḍ further on says: तस्य वा एतस्य पुरुषस्य द्वे एव स्थाने भवत इदं च परलोकस्थानं च सन्ध्यं तृतीयꣳ स्वप्नस्थानं तस्मिन्सन्ध्ये स्थाने तिष्ठन्नेते उभे स्थाने पश्यतीदं च परलोकस्थानं च . . . ॥ "There are even two places of this Purusha, this place and the place of the next world: the place of dream, which is the meeting (or middle) place (between them), is the third. Abiding in this meeting (or middle) place (Purusha or man) sees both places, this and the place of the other world."—IV, III. 9. In some versions of the above original, the word Madhyamā is used for Sandhyā.

From this it is clear that the Purusha, or Self-consciousness in average humanity, functions at present in the middle world, that of svapna or dream, the astral. How are we to reconcile this with the previous statement? In the present instance it is said we are functioning in Svapnasṭhāna, whereas in the previous Mantra it is said our consciousness is in Jāgraṭa, in the two eyes as Inḍra and Inḍrāṇī. If we go deeper, we shall be able to reconcile the two. Subdividing the three planes of Jāgraṭ, Svapna and Sushupṭi, or Bhūḥ, Bhuvaḥ and Suvaḥ, into three divisions we get the following:

First plane—Jāgraṭ or Gross body	Jāgraṭ Svapna and Sushupṭi.
Second plane—Svapna or Astral	Jāgraṭ Svapna and Sushupṭi.
Third plane—Sushupṭi or Mental	Jāgraṭ Svapna and Sushupṭi

According to this Upanishaḍ, the Purusha, though having the gross body of the first plane, functions in the second plane which is called the Svapna world. This Svapna world has its three subdivisions as above stated. Hence man's consciousness when he is performing the work of the external world functions in the Jāgraṭ of the second plane, identifying itself with the physical; in his dreaming condition is in the Svapna of the second plane; in his Sushupṭi condition is in the Sushupṭi of the same plane. This last is called in Gāyaṭrī-Viḍyā the Anṭar or inner Ākās'a. But the Bahir, or outer, Ākās'a referred to therein is the Sushupṭi of the first plane. These two Ākās'as are differentiated in the Upanishaḍ from the one which is within the Prāṇas, or network of the heart; this third Ākās'a therefore occupies a higher plane within the heart, and therefore corresponds to the Suṣhupṭi of the third plane.

In the true Rājayoga, we are asked to first meditate in the heart-centre and not on other centres. In the outer world, Yogins there are who ask us to meditate on the Ājñā-chakra, or the centre between the two eyebrows, or on the navel chakra, and so on. The mastery of the navel or Maṇipūraka centre and other centres lower down, connected with the Kuṇḍalinī therein, give us Siḍḍhis, whereas the mastery of the Ājñā-chakra enables us to go beyond the Jāgraṭ of the second plane and to develop therefore clairvoyance and other kindred powers. But true occultism is meant to develop true spirituality through the Rājayogic path, and hence asks us to go into the heart for meditation.

Here it would be well if I explain the line of thought adopted by the Upanishaḍs as to what we mean by the Purusha, or Self-consciousness in man, and as to its relationship to the Ākās'a and bodies.

It is better if we take the septenary classification and its correspondences:

LOKAS	TATTVAS	S'ARĪRAS	AVASṬHĀS	PURUSHA
Bhūḥ	Pṛṭhivī	Sṭhūla	Jāgraṭ	Vis'va
Bhuvaḥ Suvaḥ Mahaḥ	Āpas Agni Vāyu	Sūkshma	Svapna	Ṭaijasa
Janaḥ	Ākās'a	Kāraṇa	Sushupṭi	Prājna
Ṭapaḥ	Ahamkāra or Anupāḍaka	Jīva or Purusha	Ṭurīya	Ṭurīya
Saṭya	Mahaṭ or Āḍi	Hiraṇyagarbha, or Brahmā	Ṭurīyāṭīṭa	Ṭurīyāṭīṭa

In the *Sanāṭana Ḍharma* (Advanced) *Text Book*, the 5th, 6th and 7th Planes are made to correspond to the Kāraṇa S'arīra, but the Kâraṇa S'arīra corresponds strictly to the 5th plane: in the 6th plane it becomes a point or line corresponding to Buḍḍhi—the ray of Āṭmā—which becomes the all in the 7th plane. In the Purāṇas, the Mahaṭ, the Samashti, becomes the Vayshti in the Ahamkāra stage. From the above, it is clear that the Kāraṇa S'arīra begins on the 5th plane even if it does not end there; that plane corresponds to Ākās'a. Hence as said above, the three kinds of Ākās'a are no other than the Kāraṇa S'arīras which function in the different Sushupṭi states. It is this Kāraṇa S'arīra that is called either Kamala or Aṇda (lotus or egg) in the Upanishaḍs and Purāṇas. The word Pushkara is interpreted to mean Ākās'a in *Māiṭrāyaṇī-Upanishaḍ*,

In Prapāthaka v. 2 of the same, it is stated thus: कः पुष्करः किमयं वेद वा व तत्पुंष्करं योऽयमाकाशोऽस्येमाश्वतस्रो दिशश्चतस्र उपदिशः संस्थाः "What is (heart) Pushkara (or lotus)? Of what is it made? That which is Ākāśa is Pushkara. Of it, the four quarters and the four intermediate quarters are the petals." In the case of non-spiritual persons, the astral heart is like the bud of a lotus. In order to make it blossom with an upward bent, Śrī Kṛshṇa says to his beloved devotee Uddhava in *Srīmad Bhāgavata-Purāṇa*: "Uddhava said: 'O Thou having lotus eyes, it behoves Thee to describe unto me the process of meditation through which persons desirous of final liberation should meditate on Thee?' The Lord said: 'Sitting at ease on an even seat with straight body, etc., you should think of the lotus of the heart stationed inside, whose tube exists upwards and the mouth downwards, as having the mouth upwards, full-blown, with eight petals and pericarp, and should gradually think of the sun, moon and fire in the pericarp,' etc." Skandha XI, ch. XIV. *vide* for the original *The Hindū God Universal*, p. 96. Here the meditation in the pericarp on Viṣhṇu with conch, shell, etc., is prescribed. This is, if I may so call it, the artificial mode of making the lotus of the heart blossom, the meditation bringing it about. The other is the natural blooming of the heart-lotus through intense devotion. It will be evident to occult members that the latter is the course adopted in the Rajayoga School, as the heart-lotus is not meditated upon, probably because this is an age of scepticism

Again in the *Chhāndogya-Upanishad*, where the Ḍahara-Vidyā is expatiated upon, we see that the heart is treated as a lotus. The word used is Puṇḍarīka: अथ यदिदमस्मिन्ब्रह्मपुरे दहरं पुण्डरीकं वेश्म दहरोऽस्मिन्नन्तराकाशस्तस्मिन्यदन्तस्तदन्वेष्टव्यं तद्वाव विजिज्ञासितव्यमिति ॥१॥ —Aḍhyāya VIII, 1. "In this city of Brahman, there is a small lotus (as) a place; therein is the inner Ākāśa within the Ḍahara (cavity of the heart): and what is in that is to be sought after, that is to be understood." We are taught that from the plane beyond the mental, if we look at the solar system from the Ṭurīya plane, the whole of it looks like an outspread flower in space, all the petals joined at the base and the tips of the leaves representing worlds. The reason why the solar system is compared to a lotus is because it looks like a lotus to a seer; it looks like a flower outspread in space, the central Sun being its centre. "The vertical section of a tube" is also mentioned. Probably it has the form of Lotus in the concrete worlds, being nothing but the Ākāśa in the abstract state. Whether we call it lotus or egg, it dees not matter: it is the Kāraṇa Śarīra, having its centre in the heart. Before we go into an explanation of the lotus and its contents, in order to understand the Vidyās, we shall have to explain the word Purusha, or Self-consciousness, occurring in the Upanishaḍs.

PURUSHA

It is a fact known to all students of Vedānṭa, that, according to the *Māṇḍūkya-Upanishaḍ* there is an

Aḍhishṭhāna-Chaiṭanya to each of the three S'arīras, or bodies; the three consciousnesses are called Vis'va, Ṭaijasa and Prājña. We know that the one Jīvāṭmā, or Purusha, in going down into each body or plane, is given these different names. What therefore is the sub-plane of a plane into which it descends? For we all know that in the one Absolute, there is no matter to condition It. In the seventh or highest plane, the highest rarefied matter conditions It. It being the Āḍi, or Mahaṭic, plane, there is the one Lord conditioned by the one Māyā. The differentiation into many, as Ahamkāra manifests, is in the sixth sub-plane, and it is here that the Jīvas separate themselves as many. In the Theosophical literature, the ray of Āṭmā, viz., Buḍḍhi, the sixth 'Principle' comes forth from Āṭmā the seventh. In the Upanishads, the Jīvāṭmā is compared to the sparks issuing from the flame, while the *Gīṭā* compares it to a ray of light from the Sun. But in the Upanishaḍs, further descriptions are given of it; *Muṇḍaka-Upanishaḍ*, III, i. 9 says: एषोऽणुरात्मा चेतसा वेदितव्यो यस्मिन्प्राणः पञ्चधा संविवेश । "This atomic Āṭmā (soul) is to be known through Cheṭas (thinking), into which Prāṇa has entered fivefold."

Sveṭāsvaṭara v. 8, 9, says: बुद्धेर्गुणेनात्मगुणेन चैव आराग्र-मात्रोऽप्यपरोऽपि दृष्टः ॥ वालाग्रशतभागस्य शतधा कल्पितस्य च । भागो जीवः स विज्ञेयः स चानन्त्याय कल्प्यते ॥ "The lower one endowed with the quality of Buḍḍhi and with the quality of body is seen small like the point of a goad. That living Jīva is to be known as part of the hundredth part of the point of a hair, divided a hundred times, and yet it is to be known as endless."

There are other illustrations also mentioned in the Upanishaḍs, such as barley-corn, etc.

In *Yoga-Vāsishtha*, as well as in 'Purusha-Sūkṭa', it is Nīvāra-śūkavaṭ, or like the tail-end of paddy. From all these quotations, it is clear that the Jīvāṭmā is differentiated from Paramāṭmā through its limiting adjunct of the subtlest or atomic matter, which is said to be technically Aviḍyā by the Veḍānṭins. Different comparisons are made of it as the atom, a hair divided manyfold, the point of a goad, or the tail-end of paddy, to show the extreme smallness or subtlety of the Jīvāṭmā. It is this Jīvāṭmā that is indestructible. But how can it be, when it is atomic or has its limiting adjunct, which naturally should be subject to destruction? The reply is given in one of the passages above quoted. Though the Jīvāṭmā is to be known as part of the hundredth part of the point of a hair divided a hundred times, yet it is also to be known as Ananṭa or endless. It has two aspects, the lower and the higher. In the higher, it is the Infinite, but in its lower it is finite.

In *Yoga-Vāsishtha*, this very subject has been put forth from another aspect. It is correlated with Ahamkāra, as said before. There are, it says, three kinds of Ahamkāras. The first is where one identifies himself with the body, though he is intellectually convinced of the soul's existence: the second is where he identifies himself with the Nīvāra-śūka and rises above the identification with the body. The third stage is where he identifies himself with the whole universe instead of the atomic unit. In the fourth stage, he rises above the universe. All these are stages of experience. They are not matters of theory, but of direct perception. Therefore when we say the Purusha goes to this centre or that, it is this atomic unit, or Nīvāra-śūka, that moves.

Another aspect of this Purusha is stated in the sixth Praśna of *Prasnopanishaḍ* as being shodaśa-kaḷā, or sixteen-rayed. With these rays beginning from Prāṇa the Purusha forms the Kāraṇa Śarīra with its accompaniments. From Prāṇa arise śraḍḍhā, the five elements, organs, mind and food. From food arise energy, ṭapas, manṭras, karmas, and worlds, and from worlds the names (or forms). These are the different rays of Purusha going to constitute, in the lower worlds, concrete forms. This is for the purpose of meditation how the bodies, etc., arise from Jīvāṭmā.

Therefore when in meditation one habituates himself to retire into his heart in his ordinary waking state, it is this Purusha that goes into the sushupṭi-avasṭhā of the plane he is in, viz., its Kāraṇa, or Bahir (outer) Ākāśa; when the identification with the physical body ceases, he rises in meditation into the inner Ākāśa of the heart but external to the Prāṇas therein. When he rises to the sushupṭi of the third plane, he is within the Prāṇas in the inner Ākāśa of the heart. This is the shorter cut mentioned by the occultists. The purusha rises from the sushupṭi of the physical to that of the astral, and then to that of the mental—all these—in the heart.

Before we go into the centre of the lotus of the heart, we have to understand all about its outer fringe, or petals. In the second of the two chapters of the *Chhāndogya-Upanishaḍ*, treating of the Gāyaṭrī-Viḍyā, we have been given hints as to this. In the heart there are said to be five देवसुषय: or Ḍeva gates: four towards the four quarters and one upwards. At each of these gates are posted some powers. The Upanishaḍ says that if meditation is made on them in the heart, certain results ensue. Let me put it in a diagram thus:

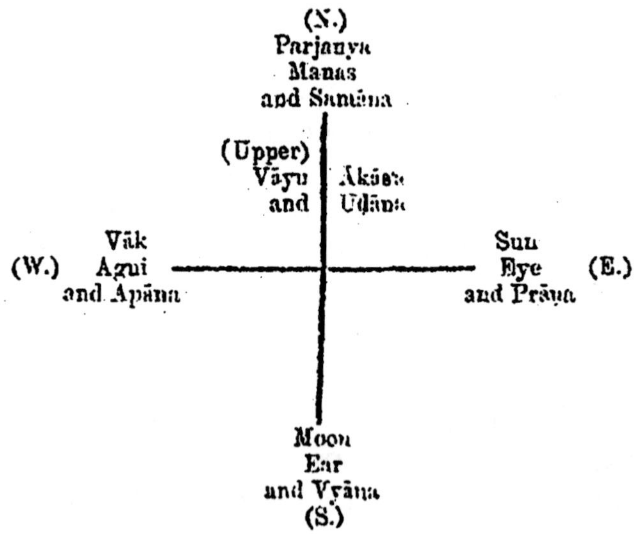

Now since the heart represents the centre of the Kāraṇa Sarīra, and as the Kāraṇa is the cause of the other lower bodies, all the germs of the organs in the lower, viz., astral and physical should be in their cause. We know that the *Māṇḍūkya-Upanishaḍ* attributes, to the Jāgraṭ and Svapna Avasṭhās and hence to the first and second bodies, nineteen Mukhas, or facets. They are explained to be the five Jñānendriyas (organs of knowledge or senses), the five Karmendriyas (organs of action), the five Prāṇas (life-breaths), and the fourfold Antaḥkarṇa (internal organ). The five organs of sense have two centres only in the causal body, *viz.*, the eye and the ear: the first two organs of smell and taste being merged into that of sight, and the organ of touch into that of hearing. As these organs are correlated to the five elements, Pṛthivī and Āpas become merged into Agni, and Vāyu into Ākāsa. In the Karmendriyas, Vāk alone remains: the Antaḥkaraṇa is taken as one only. In the upper gate there is Vāyu to unify them as one. In sushupti, the Aḍhishthāna Ḍevas of the organs do not work in them, but retire into their respective centres in the heart as before stated. Though there are the organs in the lower plane, they are unable to function on account of the Prāṇa and the Chaitanya having been withdrawn into the higher. In the Major Upanishaḍs, such as *Kena*, we find the eye and ear alone mentioned as the organs of sense. Why? Since they alone exist as potential centres in the kāraṇa condition. So also with reference to the other organs. This is with reference to Āḍhyāṭmic or human standpoint. According to Ḍahara-Viḍyā all the worlds are in the heart, corresponding to the human divisions. The Sun is the gate for the first world: the Moon for the second: Agni for the third; Parjanya for the fourth: and Ākās'a for the fifth. If we imagine the worlds as concentric circles therein, we have the gate of the first world on the east of the heart, through the Sun, and similarly with reference to the other gates. The Sun stands for Pṛṭhivī: the Moon for Āpas: Vāk for Agni and Parjanya for Vāyu.

Coming to the Prāṇas, we find that Prāṇa and Apāna are positive and negative, and hence are posted in the opposite gates, east and west; their functions being inspiration and expiration. Vyāna is the neutral or Laya point of the two. As S'rī S'aṅkara puts it: It is the Sanḍhi (connecting point) of Prāṇa and Apānā striving for Kumbhak, and does all actions involving expenditure of energy. Whenever actions are performed which involve expenditure of energy, such as jumping, etc., we have to control the breath: inspiration and expiration meeting therein. Samāna is that which carries all the rasas (or chyle) of the food digested to all the parts of the body. Prāṇa and Apāna corresponding to Pṛṭhivī and Agni, Samāna corresponds to water. Hence it is in the middle point of the two connected with Vyāna as its antipodes. Samāna expanding and Vyāna contracting, they are at the opposite poles of the central point of Prāṇa and Apāna. Uḍāna is at the higher point, as it performs the function of taking upward and unifying all the Prāṇas into one, and taking up the Jiva to the higher worlds. It is the cause of all Karmas which tend to go up. In the Upanishaḍ, it is compared to a fisherman, who casts his net in the waters, and after catching the fish draws the net together as one unto himself. In the upper gate, the Uḍāna is merged into Vāyu (the Samashti) which again merges into Ākāsa. Thus therefore when, in the Viḍyās enunciated above, the Upāsaka is asked to meditate upon the elements, Sun, Moon or another, he should meditate upon them in the heart. Take the eastern gate. He should meditate upon the eye and its counterpart in the Universe, the Sun. The Prāṇa also should be meditated upon there. Then it is said in the Gāyaṭrī-Viḍyā that he would become full of Ṭejas and be able to consume or digest food. As regards the other gates, *viz.*, south, west, north and upper, the meditation upon them generates the following results respectively (1) prosperity and fame, (2) divine effulgence and digestion of food (3) reputation and beauty; (4) glory and strength.

Beyond these five gate-keepers, who make heroes to be born in the family of him that knows them and bestow heaven on them, there is the Supreme Light, which is the same as that which shines glorious above yonder heaven, above this world and above all others, large and small. It is here the individual soul is led to the Supreme Soul beyond the gate-keepers. This is called the Viḍyā of Paramjyoṭis but it is only a part of Gāyaṭrī-Viḍyā. Hence the *Chhānḍogya* says in another place thus: एवमेवैष संप्रसादोऽस्माच्छरीरात्समुत्थाय परं ज्योतिरुपसंपद्य स्वेन रूपेणाभिनिष्पद्यते . . . ॥

"Even like unto them, the soul through samprasāḍa (serenity or peace) issues forth from its body, attains the Paramjyoṭis, and assumes its own genuine state" —VIII, xii. 3.

The heart is described in the Upanishaḍs in other ways. It is said to be a lotus of eight petals or twelve petals. In the latter case, it is that which is located in the Sūkshma or subtle body. In that subtle body, are said to be different Chakras or wheels; or Paḍmas or lotuses. The Mūlāḍhāra, the first of which is situated at the base of the spinal column and hence is called its Mūlāḍhāra, or primal support, is endowed with four petals. Similarly one centre after another has its own number of petals, till we come to the Anāhaṭa Chakra in the heart where it is said to be twelve-petalled; the 12 petals having their functions of generating the letters of the Samskṛit consonants from क onwards or colour, etc. But the eight petals are described more in the Upanishaḍs, as the centre to which the soul goes in sleep. According to its tendency, it goes to one or other of the petals therein. The heart of eight petals is probably situated in the lower subdivision of the third world. The eight petals may also refer to the directions, cardinal and ordinal. But in the subject of Viḍyas with which we are concerned, these aspects of form are unnecessary. We are concerned with the meditation in the Kāraṇa Śarīra which is in the higher subdivisions of the third world and from which the disciple has to rise. Hence it is probably that none of the Viḍyas makes mention of the different centres of the astral heart in svapna or dream or the eight petals. Therefore only the four gates of the heart together with the upper gate which forms the fifth, wherein are posted the different powers are necessary for us. We may proceed to understand the different Viḍyas. Only it is the Gâyaṭrī-Viḍya, as explained in the third Aḍhyāya of *Chhānḍogya-Upanishaḍ*, that furnishes us with the key to unravel the mysteries connected with the different Viḍyas.

AKSHI-VIḌYĀ

In the eastern gate of the heart, are posted the gate-keepers of the eye, the sun and Prāṇa. Let us first take up the Viḍyā relating to the eye. *Chhānḍogya* IV, xv. 1 says: य एषोऽक्षिणि पुरुषो दृश्यत एष आत्मेति होवाचैतदमृतमभयमेतद्ब्रह्मेति तद्यद्यप्यस्मिन्सर्पिर्वोदकं वा सिञ्चन्ति वर्त्मनी एव गच्छति ॥ "That being who is seen within the eyes is verily the soul, said (the tutor). He is deathless or fearless. He is Brahman. Should any ghee or water drop on Him, that passeth away." In the Akshi-Viḍyā, the meditation is not external but only internal. We are not asked to meditate upon the external eye but upon the Purusha in it which is no other than our soul. This Purusha as has been already remarked is that which functions in the waking condition. In the *Bṛhadāraṇyaka* quotation given above, we find that in the Jāgraṭ the Purusha has two aspects, Indra and his wife Indrāṇī or Virāṭ who are made to preside over the right and left eyes respectively. Hence it is that both these that have to be conjointly meditated upon. If meditated in the heart, one is led to the Sushupṭi state: but in the two eyes visible in the body, then one is led beyond the Jāgraṭ only. That soul is said to be Brahman himself. Through this meditation, one is led to Brahman or Saguṇa Brahman. Through this meditation, the Amānava-Purusha above alluded to takes the devotee through the Ḍevayāna path to Saguṇa Brahman. What are the results of this Viḍyā? They are three in number, Saṃyaḍvāma, Vāmanī (receptacle) and Bhāmanī (effulgence). In the first and second cases, all adorable objects (Vāma) merge into him, he being the receptacle and in the last case, he becomes effulgent everywhere.

ANTARĀDITYA-VIDYĀ

In order to correlate them, viz., the eye and the sun, its counterpart in the universe, there is a passage in *Bṛhadāraṇyaka*, V, v. 2. तद्यत्तत्सत्यमसौ स आदित्यो य एष एतस्मिन्मण्डले पुरुषो यश्चायं दक्षिणेऽक्षन्पुरुषस्तावेतावन्योन्यस्मिन्प्रतिष्ठितौ रश्मिभिरेषोऽस्मिन्प्रतिष्ठितः प्राणैरयममुष्मिन् स यदोत्क्रमिष्यन्भवति शुद्धमेवैतन्मण्डलं पश्यति नैनमेते रश्मयः प्रत्यायन्ति ॥

"That Satya is Āditya, the Purusha dwelling in that orb and also the Purusha (dwelling) in the right eye. They abide in each other. The former abides through his rays in the latter (by the manifestation of objects); and the latter in the former through his senses (or perception). When he quits the body, he beholds that pure orb (viz., the moon); the rays do return to him." Hence in order to effectually perform the Akshi-Vidyā, its counterpart in the cosmos or Solar system has to be taken up; only when the two are correlated and meditated upon, there will be conscious acting in both. Otherwise through the Akshi-Vidyā alone, there will be but an unconscious acting through the eye with but selfish results. Hence the meditation in Akshi-Vidyā is to be carried on in the eastern gate of the heart, with Purusha of the right eye, viz., Indra to be correlated with the Purusha of the Sun, as after death or otherwise the former becomes merged into the latter.

Āḍiṭya-Viḍyā

The Āḍiṭya-Viḍyā is mentioned in the *Chhānḍogya-Upanishaḍ* I, vi. 6 and 7 thus: अथ यदेवैतदादित्यस्य शुक्लं भाः सैव साथ यन्नीलं परः कृष्णं तदमस्तत्सामाथ य एषोऽन्तरादित्ये हिरण्मयः पुरुषो दृश्यते हिरण्यश्मश्रुर्हिरण्यकेश आप्रणखात्सर्व एव सुवर्णः ॥ तस्य यथा कप्यासं पुण्डरीकमेवमक्षिणी तस्योदिति नाम स एष सर्वेभ्यः पाप्मभ्य उदित उदेति ह वै सर्वेभ्यः पाप्मभ्यो य एवं वेद ॥

"Verily, the white brightness (light) of the sun is Sa; that which is Nila (blue)—very black—is ama whence comes Sāma. That resplendent Purusha of golden hair and whiskers whose whole body even unto the nails is of gold, whom we behold in the interior of the sun and whose eyes are like lotuses red as the posteriors of a monkey is called Uṭ. He verily is above (Uḍgaṭa) all sin. He indeed ascends above all sin who knows him thus."

Therefore one who realises the Āḍiṭya Purusha through the above Viḍyā is able to rise above all sin and eventually reach Saguṇa Brahman. Here the word 'Saṭya' may be noted as used in the aforesaid *Bṛhaḍāraṇyaka-Upanishaḍ*. It is composed of three Aksharas or syllables: स, ति and य. The first and the last are said to be truth, while the middle one is said to be Anṛṭa or falsehood, the falsehood being thus encompassed by truth on either side. If the Solar system be divided into three regions, naturally the middle or Svapna world is one of falsehood. In correlating the Purusha of the eye with that* of the universe, the meditation is also thus :

य एष एतस्मिन्मण्डले पुरुषस्तस्य भूरिति शिर एकꣳशिर एकमेतदक्षरं भुव इति बाहू द्वौ बाहू द्वे एते अक्षरे स्वरिति प्रतिष्ठा द्वे प्रतिष्ठे द्वे एते अक्षरे तस्योपनिषदहरिति हन्ति पाप्मानं जहाति च य एवं वेद ॥

योऽयं दक्षिणेऽक्षन्पुरुषस्तस्य भूरिति शिर एकꣳशिर एकमेतदक्षरं भुव इति बाहू द्वौ बाहू द्वे एते अक्षरे स्वरिति प्रतिष्ठा प्रतिष्ठे द्वे द्वे एते अक्षरे तस्योपनिषदहमिति हन्ति पाप्मानं जहाति च य एवं वेद ॥

—*Bṛhaḍāraṇyaka-Upanishaḍ*, V, v. 3, 4.

" Bhūḥ is the head of the Purusha, dwelling in that orb of the sun, there being one head and also one Akshara—Bhuvaḥ, the arms—there being two arms and also two syllables—Suvaḥ, the foundation—there being two foundations and also two syllables. His representative name is Ahar (day); whoever thus knows, destroys (hanṭi) and relinquishes (Jahāṭi) sin. " Bhūḥ is the head of the Purusha dwelling in the right eye, there being one head and also one Akshara—Bhuvaḥ, the arms—there being two arms and also two syllables—Suvaḥ, the foundation—there being two foundations and also two syllables. His representative name is Aham; for whoever thus knows, destroys and relinquishes sin :

Thus Akshi- and Anṭarāḍiṭya-Viḍyas may be combined as one.

MADHU-VIDYĀ

As Madhu-Vidyā is connected with the sun, I have taken it up here. It should not be confounded with the Madhu-Brāhmaṇa or chapter in the *Bṛhadāraṇyaka,* II, v. where Dadhīchi, son of Atharvan explained to the two As'vins at his own peril this Madhu or honey, as being in all objects through the Ātmā in them. The Madhu-Vidyā is explained in *Chhāndogya,* Adhyāya III, from Khāṇḍa I. to XI. In the first Khanda, the sun is said to be the Madhu or honey of all Devas. Here certain descriptions are given, which have to be entered into. Adhyāya III, Khanda I. runs thus:

ॐ असौ वा आदित्यो देवमधु तस्य द्यौरेव तिरश्चीनवꣳशोऽन्तरिक्षमपूपो मरीचयः पुत्राः ॥१॥ तस्य ये प्राञ्चो रश्मयस्ता एवास्य प्राच्यो मधुनाड्य ऋच एष मधुकृत ऋग्वेद एष पुष्पं ता अमृता आपस्ता वा एता ऋचः ॥२॥ एतमृग्वेदमभ्यतपꣳस्तस्याभितप्तस्य यशस्तेज इन्द्रियं वीर्यमन्नाद्यꣳ रसोऽजायत ॥३॥ तद्व्यक्षरत्तदादित्यमभितोऽश्रयत्तद्वा एतद्यदेतदादित्यस्य रोहितꣳरूपम् ॥४॥

"Om, verily Āditya, the sun is the Madhu (honey) of the Devas; Dyau (heaven) is the Tiras'chīnavams'aḥ; Antariksha is hive (or honeycomb); Marīchayaḥ (the rays) are the eggs of the sun; the eastern beams are the eastern honey cells. The Ṛgvedas form the flowers; and the waters are the nectars. Verily those

Ṛk hymns made Ṭapas upon the Ṛgveḍa. Out of them arose fame, Ṭapas, the organs, energy, food and other like essences. They flowed and rested round the sun. Verily thence proceedeth the redness of the sun." Similarly other directions of the sun are taken up viz., the southern, western, northern and upper, to which are attached the Veḍas, Yajur, Sāma and Aṭharvaṇa as well as Brahma with the rays arising of colours white, dark, very dark and Kshobhaṭā (quivering light) in the centre of the sun. Then from the sixth section onwards, the different Ḍevas who enjoy the nectar at each direction of the sun are described as Vasus with Agni at their head, Rudras with Inḍra, Āḍiṭyas with Varuṇa, Maruṭs with Soma and lastly Sāḍhyas with Brahmā at their head.

Then in Khaṇda XI. it is stated that beyond these there is neither rising nor setting, but there is the remaining alone at the centre : अथ तत ऊर्ध्वं उदेत्य नैवोदेता नास्तमेतैकल एव मध्ये स्थाता . . . ॥१॥

From the above quotation, it appears that the third world is described as Ṭiras'chīnavams'aḥ and the second world as honeycomb. The word Ṭiras'chīnavams'aḥ is translated by some as "arched bamboo" and by others as "cross beam". I prefer the latter. Why should the second and the third worlds appear as such in the solar system? We all know that the three worlds are like eggs in space, the higher expanding beyond its lower. According to the description of the 2nd and 3rd worlds as found in the *Vishṇu-Purāṇa,* both have their central axis in the sun, the 2nd being between the sun and the earth and the third being between the Sun and the Ḍhruva (polar star). It may be thus:

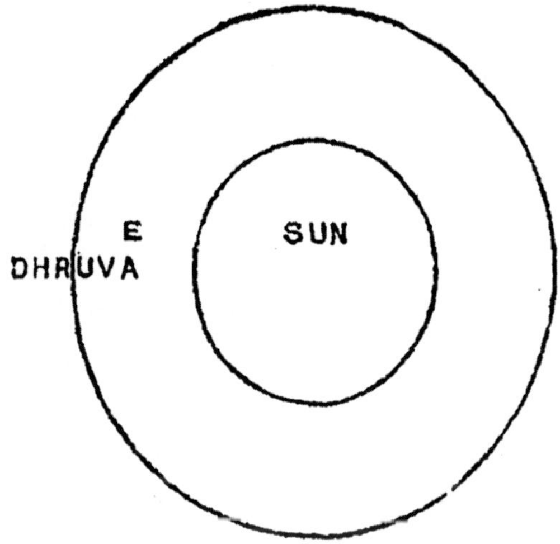

Probably when one is in the second world, he sees the third world which is away from him as an arched bamboo or cross-beam. The cross-beam probably represents the axis of activity—called warp and woof—seen in the 3rd world supporting the 2nd. Just as we, in the physical world, see the sky as a vault above, so also the third may be seen as an arch from the 2nd world that is seen hanging in space like an egg or honey-comb. Just as a honeycomb hangs from an arched beam tied to it, so the 2nd world seems to be attached to the upper through the Vāyu or prāṇic cord, as the central axis. The Purusha of the sun is located in the second world, like the soul of men functioning ordinarily in the second body. The Purusha is not the second world itself, as our soul is not the astral body itself. The soul functions in the body as its madhu, or honey. Āditya—the Purusha—is therefore the honey in that world to the Devas living there. The Devas do not drink the honey, but through the mere sight are gratified, just as those in the moon are pleased through the mere sight of nectar.

As regards the cells in the honeycomb, they are constructed on a geometrical basis. The whole Universe is a four-phased hexagonal solid. Each cell is Hexagon on its sides. If we go into the geometrical plan of the universe as dedncible from the Upanishads, it seems as if the bees had intuitively understood the plan of the universe and reproduced it in the honeycomb. The great Sages in comparing the universe to the honeycomb did not accidentally hit upon this simile but were able to intuit through their higher vision the correspondence.

Then in many sections, the analogy of the honeycomb is carried on. In the different directions of east, south, west, north and zenith, are said to be the Vedas, Ṛg, Yajus, Sāma and Atharva Āṅgīras (Itihāsas and Purāṇas) and Brahmā (with his guhya or occult teachings). The colours are respectively, red, white, dark, very dark, and Kshobhaṭā in the middle. As stated in another place, the very dark colour is but Indigo or dark blue. Of the Devas, the Vāsus with Agni at their head are in the east; the Rudras with Indra, in the south; Ādityas with Varuṇa, in the west; Maruts with Soma in the north and Sādhyas with Brahmā (Om) above. Beyond these in the centre is said to be the one Saṭya which has neither setting nor rising. He who knows the

Ḍevas in the sun as partakers of the honey becomes himself one of them and partakes in it himself. The hymns of the respective Vedas, etc., are said to be the bees or manufacturers of the honey of the sun, viz., out of the Vedas or the Iṭihāsas and Purāṇas or the Guhya Teachings. In other words, the sounds of all the Vedas uttered rhythmically generate the body or orb of the sun in the different directions. In this connection we may quote the following:

"As studied by H. P. B., a page of the book (of Dzyan) would be taken and placed in contact with the hand or forehead. It is most powerfully magnetised, so that the person thus using it sees unrolled before him a cosmic picture; the events as it were taking place before his eyes. In seeing the pictures thus, there is a great stimulation of faculty at the same time; the pupil hears the most marvellous music of the spheres. There is at once a picture and a chant." Similarly when the sun had to be created, the honey in the eastern cells, viz., the sun in the east was generated out of the chanting of Ṛks of the Ṛgveḍa; that in the south, out of the Yajus; that in the west, out of the Sāma; that in the north, out of Iṭihāsas and Purāṇas through the Ṭapas upon them of Aṭharva Āṅgiras: and that in the upper through the Ṭapas of Brahmā out of the Guhya or occult teachings. In the course of the Ṭapas, there were generated as results, Yaśas (fame) Ṭejas, etc., which, it is said, flowed to the sun and rested there. In the honeycomb, there are in the cells not only honey but also eggs hatched by the bees in order to have more bees to generate honey. These eggs are said to be the Marichayaḥ or rays. The Veḍic hymns when uttered generate the orb of the sun which in turn sends out its ray, viz., other hymns Thus a person who goes in for meditation upon the sun as the Maḍhu or honey will be able to drink the honey like the Ḍevas who are there—which honey is differentiated by the different directions in which it is. If from this the Upāsaka or devotee wishes to rise to Nirguṇa Brahman, he has to rise beyond the central portion of the sun where Brahmā is stated to be the Saguṇa with His Kshobhaṭā —the māyāvic light existing there.

PURUSHA-VIḌYĀ

In this Viḍyā, are introduced the above Ḍevas Vasus, Ruḍras, etc. *Veḍānṭa-Sūṭras* make mention of it in III, III. 2; but it does not find a place in the list of the 32 Viḍyās above enumerated. In this Viḍyā man is represented as a Yājña or Sacrificer. In the *Ṭaiṭṭirīya-Āraṇyaka*, x. 64 it is stated thus:

तस्यैवं विदुषो यज्ञस्याऽऽत्मा यजमानः श्रद्धा पत्नी

"For him who knows thus, the Āṭmā of the sacrifice is the Master, Sraḍḍhā is the wife of the sacrificer, etc." In the *Chhānḍogya*, III, XVI. also, the Purusha is described as a Yājña in other ways. The question taken up for discussion in *Veḍānṭa-Sūṭras* is whether the above two Purusha-Viḍyās can be combined as one in meditation. The reply is in the negative, as the particulars contained in them differ. Coming to the Purusha-Viḍyā of *Chhānḍogya*, we find man's life is divided into three portions. The first lasts for 24 years and therefore the morning ritual (Pṛāṭaḥ-savana) is done with the Gāyaṭrī metre of 24 syllables in all—each verse being of six syllables—with the Vasus as the Ḍevaṭās; should any disease afflict him within this age, he is asked to recite the manṭra therein prescribed addressed to the Vasus in Gāyaṭrī metre. Thus he escapes from disease and becomes exempt from affliction. The next savana is of 20 years till the 44th year and is called the Māḍhyanḍinam or noon-savana. The Manṭra is addressed to the Ruḍras with Ṭṛshtup metre of 44 syllables—each verse of 11 syllables. The same results of freedom from disease and affliction ensue. The third savana is of 40 years till the 84th year and dedicated to the Āḍiṭyas. Here the Manṭra to be addressed to them is in Jagaṭī metre of 48 syllables—each verse of 12 syllables. एतद्ध स्म वै तद्विद्वानाह महिदास ऐतरेयः स किं म एतदुपतपसि योऽहमनेन न प्रेष्यामीति स ह षोडशं वर्षशतमजीवत्प्रह षोडशं वर्षशतं जीवति य एवं वेद ॥७॥ "Verily knowing this, Mahiḍāsa Aiṭareya said: 'Oh, why dost thou afflict me? For I shall not be destroyed by thee. He lived for 116 years'. Verily he will live for 116 years who knoweth this." For the Manṭras to be addressed to Vasus, Ruḍras and Āḍiṭyas, the reader is asked to refer to the original Upanishaḍ. In the first period of man's life, the Vasus are the presiding deity; hence the Prāṇa tending towards life is with the Vasus. The Vasus (vāsayanṭi) preserve men: similarly Ruḍras in the second portion of life—corresponding to the household life—(roḍayanṭi or) make them weep under the sufferings of the household. The third portion of life tending towards spirituality, the Āḍiṭyas (āḍaḍaṭe or) receive all things as experiences.

PRĀṆA- AND PRATARḌANA-VIḌYĀS

THERE is yet a third element in the eastern gate, viz., Prāṇa; but in order to dispose of it, we have to take all the Prāṇas together. Prāṇāgnihoṭra-Viḍyā deals with them all. It deals not only with Prāṇa but also with Agni which is posted at the western gate or the third. The second or southern gate has no viḍyā appurtenant to it alone—there being in it the moon and ear with Vyāna. The reason why no separate meditation is prescribed with reference to it is probably because it is a gate of Yama and the Sanḍhi or meeting point of Prāṇa and Apāna. In the *Chhānḍogya-Upanishaḍ*, prāṇa-viḍyā is dealt with in Aḍhyāya I, XI. Ushasṭi Chākrāyaṇa, an Āṭmajñānin goes to a sacrifice with his wife and tells the Uḍgāṭṛ and others that if they should chant in praise of Him who is the presiding deity without knowing His nature, their heads would be lopped off or splintered to pieces. Thereon the sacrifice was stopped and the master of the sacrifice, the king who was sent for arrived at the spot and after satisfying the Great One with presents etc., requested him to initiate the priests into their respective mysteries. As regards the Aḍhvaryu, he was initiated into his part as having prāṇa for his Ḍevaṭā. "Verily all these created objects merge into Prāṇa and from it they are developed." This Viḍyā is dealt with *in extenso* in the second and third Aḍhyāyas of *Kaushīṭakī*. The third Aḍhyāya comes under the category of Praṭarḍana-Viḍyā, since Praṭarḍana was initiated into it by Inḍra. In the first Aḍhyāya, prāṇa is made the couch of Brahmā of unmeasured splendour—Amiṭaujasam—Paryaṅkam which will be dealt with under the heading of Paryaṅka-Viḍyā, In the second Aḍhyāya, Prāṇa is said to be Brahman itself. Of course the Mukhya or chief Prāṇa which includes in it all the five Prāṇas is said to be the highest of all. The word Prāṇas is also made to mean the senses. We are perfectly familiar with the story occurring again and again in the Upanishaḍs how disputes arose between all the senses in the body including that legitimately called the Prāṇa, as regards the superiority of one over the other and how each Inḍriya or sense went out of the body and yet others were able to function in its absence and how when the Mukhya Prāṇa—Prāṇa, the legitimate one went out, all the other senses had to be wrenched away from the body along with it. In the second Aḍhyāya, Prāṇa, the Mukhya, is shown to be superior and to be guiding Manas, eye, ear, Vāk and others. Manas is said to be the messenger; eye, the guard; ear, the door-keeper; Vāk, the true woman. In another place Vāk is said to be the wife of Prāṇa, which is the deity of deities. In the third Aḍhyāya of Praṭarḍana-Viḍyā, Prāṇa is associated with Prājña, the Purusha presiding over the third body or Avasṭhā;

and from that we are to rise in meditation to Brahman. It is needless to state that if meditation is carried on in the heart on the different Prāṇas in the different gates, certain siddhis arise. In *Pataññjali's Yoga-Sūtras*, it is said that if Samyama is made upon Samāna, then a certain Jvalanam or blazing, as if, of fire takes place in the body. This is more easily done by meditating upon Samāna in the northern gate of the heart. Perhaps the meditation has to be associated with the raising of the Kuṇḍalinī from the navel to the northern gate of the heart. Similarly with reference to the other Prāṇas in the other gates.

PRĀṆĀGNIHOTRA-VIḌYA

We come to the particulars of meditation with reference to the different Prāṇas in this Vidyâ. In the 32 Vidyās mentioned above, this Vidyā is classed under the category of Vaisvānara-Vidyā which is different from the Vaisvānarāgni that is mentioned in *Bṛhadāraṇyaka*, V, IX. thus: अयमग्निर्वैश्वानरो योऽयमन्तः पुरुषे येनेदमन्नं पच्यते यदिदमद्यते तस्यैष घोषो भवति यमेतत्कर्णावपिधाय शृणोति स यदोत्क्रमिष्यन्भवति नैनं घोषं शृणोति ॥१॥

"The fire whose name is Vaisvānara is that fire in the midst of the body by which all the food that is eaten is digested. From this Agni (fire), arises a noise which one hears in closing his ears. When he (the soul) quits the body, he does not hear the noise." This is only one of the three fires in the body. The first is called, in the *Garbhopanishad*, Koshtha or Vaisvānara; the second Jñānāgni and the third, Ḍarsanāgni. They are posted in the Mūlāḍhāra (Sacral plexus), the heart and the eyes. They have their counterparts in the universe. They are Pāvaka, Pavamāna and Suchi. In the Vidyā now under consideration, only one Agni is taken into consideration along with the five Prāṇas separately.

Prāṇāgnihotra is dealt with in six sections beginning with section XIX. of the fifth Aḍhyāya of *Chhānḍogya*. Practically the oblation to the five Prāṇas has to be done daily by the Ḍvijas, when they take the food. With first oblation of the first mouthful, they have to utter the words: प्राणाय स्वाहा ॥ with the second, व्यानाय स्वाहा ॥ with the third, अपानाय स्वाहा ॥ with the fourth, समानाय स्वाहा ॥ with the fifth, उदानाय स्वाहा ॥ In the concluding section, we are told that he who performs Agnihoṭra without knowing the above has the same reward as he who forsaking burning coals pours his oblation upon ashes; but if he should do it knowingly, then his sins will be burnt like reed-tops cast on fire. 'Therefore verily were he, who knows, to offer the remnant of his food (even) to a Chaṇḍāla, he would effect an offering to the All-pervading Āṭmā.' Thereof is the verse: यथेह क्षुधिता बाला मातरं पर्युपासते। एवꣳसर्वाणि भूतान्यग्निहोत्रमुपासत इत्यग्निहोत्रमुपासत इति ॥

"As in common life hungry children look to their mothers, so do all the creatures look up to Agni-hoṭra—verily they look up to Agnihoṭra."—*Chhānḍogya*, V, XXIV. 5.

Daily while eating, we utter the five Prāṇas as mentioned above and with each uttering take in a small quantity of food with the tips of the three fingers. And in order to lead us to Brahman from that stage, we utter also the words as before: ब्रह्मणे स्वाहा ॥ ब्रह्मणि म आत्मामृतत्वाय ॥

Now in the passages relating to this Viḍyā, it is said that if the words प्राणाय स्वाहा are uttered, the eye and the sun and thereby the Ḍyau (Heaven) are satisfied; with the second, the ear and the moon and thereby the Ḍik (quarters): with the third, Vāk and Agni and thereby Pṛṭhivī; with the fourth, the Manas and Parjanya and thereby Viḍyuṭ (Lightning); with the fourth, Vāyu and Ākās'a and all that depend on them are satisfied. So far as the organs in man and their counterparts in the cosmos are concerned, they conform strictly to the statement about the heart-gate-keepers in the Gāyaṭrī-Viḍyā. But there is one step more to be taken. The elements corresponding to them are also here given. One difficulty presents itself. Instead of making the first or the eastern gate correspond to Pṛṭhivī and the third or its opposite gate to Agni, the reverse is adopted. And why? For this purpose we shall have to quote another passage from the *Chhāndogya*, IV, XVII.

प्रजापतिर्लोकानभ्यतपत्तेषां तप्यमानानाꣳ रसान्प्रावृहदग्निं पृथिव्या वायुमन्तरिक्षादादित्यं दिवः ॥१॥

"Prajāpaṭi made a Ṭapas on Lokas; and out of the Ṭapas, extracted their essence, viz., Agni from Pṛṭhivī, Vāyu from Anṭariksha and Āḍiṭya from Ḍyau (Heaven)". Hence Agni is the essence or Rasa of the first world and the Sun is the essence of the third. Thus it is clear that if one should knowingly before taking food go into his heart gates and mentally utter the Manṭras corresponding to the respective Prāṇas, the different organs are kept in a healthy condition in the lower states too; thus if the Kāraṇa body is acted upon, the lower states should thereby be affected.

Then the devotee has to rise beyond the five Prāṇas to Brahman as stated before. Here I have to make mention of two Mantras which are uttered both before and after taking food. One is uttered before the five Prāṇas are uttered, viz., अमृतोपस्तरणमसि and the other, अमृतापिधानमसि. On both occasions, water is sipped with the uttering. Through the first Manṭra the water is made the उपस्तरणं or bed on which the food is laid and in the other, the water is made the अपिधानं or upper covering for the food.

UḌGĪṬHA-VIḌYĀ

Coming to the third gate, we have Agni and Vāk. Regarding the latter, we have the Uḍgīṭha-Viḍyā But Vāk itself has no Viḍyā allotted to it. It is described as a milch-cow with four udders in *Bṛhaḍ-āraṇyaka*, V, VIII.

वाचं धेनुमुपासीत तस्याश्चत्वारः स्तनाः स्वाहाकारो वषट्कारो हन्तकारः स्वधाकारस्तस्य द्वौ स्तनौ देवा उपजीवन्ति स्वाहाकारं च वषट्कारं च हन्तकारं मनुष्याः स्वधाकारं पितरस्तस्याः प्राण ऋषभो मनो वत्सः ॥१॥

"Let one meditate on speech (as) Ḍhenu (milch-cow). Her four udders are the words "Svāhā", "Vashat", "Hanṭa" and "Svaḍhā". Two udders the words, Svāhā and Vashat feed the Ḍevas; the word, Hanṭa feeds men; the word, Svaḍhā, the Piṭṛs. Her bull is Prāṇa; and the calf is Manas. *Chhānḍogya* makes them a Miṭhuna or Couple. Thus Prāṇa acting upon Vāk generates Manas; Vāk is fourfold: Parā, Pas'yanṭī, Maḍhyamā and Vaikharī. In the Uḍgīṭha-Viḍyā, these four stages of Vāk are mentioned. Even in the Gāyaṭrī-Viḍyā, Vāk is the first thing mentioned to render it effective, as all manṭras have to be rendered effective through it. The Uḍgīṭha-Viḍyā is treated of in the Sāmaveḍa Upanishaḍs as Uḍgīṭha and in other Upanishaḍs as

Praṇava. The question arises in the *Veḍānṭa-Sūṭras* whether they are different Viḍyās or the same. All are one Viḍyā only is the reply. In the *Chhānḍogya Upanishaḍ*, the first Mantra is : ओमित्येतदक्षरमुद्गीथमुपासीत "Let a man meditate upon this letter (Om), Uḍgīṭha." Similarly the *Māṇḍūkya-Upanishaḍ* treats of this wholly. The different svaras of Uḍgīṭha are not mentioned in the important Upanishaḍs. But we find from other Upanishaḍs that there are different svaras to it. In *Nāraḍuparivrājaka-Upanishaḍ*, it is stated to have many svaras. But it is too big a subject to be treated here.

NĀCHIKEṬA-AGNI-VIḌYĀ

As stated in the *Kathopanishaḍ*, when Nachikeṭas went to Yama, the second boon that was granted to him was the knowledge of the Heavenly fire, viz., the fire of the third world. Its corresponding seat in the human body is said to be the cavity of the heart. Beyond knowing that this Agni has been called by his name and that if the third Agni were known the two lower worlds would be known, we are in the dark as regards other points. But if we go into the next Viḍyā, we are able to know something more.

UPAKOSALA-VIḌYĀ

UPAKOSALA KAMALĀYANA was a disciple of Saṭyakāma Jābāla who also has a viḍyā after his name. He tended carefully for 12 years the Agni of his guru as a pure Brahmachārin. When the time to give leave to his pupils came, all were given permission to return home except Upakosala. In spite of the entreaties of his wife, the guru neither initiated the pupil nor gave leave to him but went on a pilgrimage. In his absence, the disciple fell ill and abstained from food on account of his mental troubles. The master's wife prevailed upon him to take some nourishment but in vain. Then the Agnis began to commiserate his pitiable plight and initiated him into the secrets. All the Agnis, collectively and separately, imparted to him the truths, till at last the Guru returned from his pilgrimage and gave the final touch by teaching the Akshi-Viḍyā already spoken of. This occurs in *Chhānḍogga,* IV, x. to xv.

We shall take them in order. All the Agnis together said first: प्राणो ब्रह्म कं ब्रह्म खं ब्रह्मेति—*Chhānḍogya,* IV, x. 5. "Prāṇa is Brahman; Kam (happiness) is Brahman; Kham (Ākās') is Brahman." Then Gārhapaṭya Agni instructed him thus: अथ हैनं गार्हपत्योऽनुशशास पृथिव्यग्निरन्नमादित्य इति य एष आदित्ये पुरुषो दृश्यते सोऽहमस्मि स एवाहमस्मीति ॥ स य एतमेवं विद्वानुपास्तेऽपहते पापकृत्यां लोकीभवति सर्वमायुरेति ज्योग्जीवति नास्यावरपुरुषाः क्षीयन्त उप वयं तं भुञ्जामोऽस्मिꣳश्च लोकेऽमुष्मिꣳश्च य एतमेवं विद्वानुपास्ते ॥—*Chhānḍogya,* IV, xi. 1, 2.

"Pṛthivī Agni, Anna (food) and Āḍiṭya (are my body). Thereof the Purusha that is seen in the sun is I—verily I am He. He destroyeth the sin who knowing this adoreth Him; he attaineth the region (of Agni), enjoyeth the full limit of existence, passeth his life in glory and his race wasteth not. We support in this and Higher lokas who knowing this makes an Upāsanā of him . . . ." Then Anvāhāryapachana fire said similarly with this difference: Āpas, Ḍik, Nakshaṭra and Chanḍramāḥ (moon) are my body; myself being the Purusha in the moon. The third fire Āhavanīya said: "Prāṇa, Ākās', Ḍyau and Viḍyuṭ (are my body); myself being the Purusha in the Viḍyuṭ (lightning)." After he was instructed thus, the guru returned from his pilgrimage and finding that his disciple was beaming with divine effulgence asked the reason; to which the S'ishya replied that he was instructed by the Agnis. The teacher said that the Agnis had instructed him merely about the attaining of the different lokas stated therein. For which purpose, he asked his disciple to take up the corresponding centre in the body, viz., the eyes in the heart as stated before. Of the three fires in man, as I have already stated, that in the stomach is here described as Gārhapaṭya (corresponding to the first world or loka); the second, to the second loka; the third, to the third loka; the Agni being here described from the standpoint of the Lokas or Worlds: Hence the meditation upon them leads to the worlds therein described. If we go into the Ḍevayāna path, we are led to the Agni loka through these meditations: the Agni loka being the first loka to which one is led by the Amānava-Purusha after the latter meets the former. All of them said collectively that collective meditation led the devotee to Prāṇa and Ākās'a which typified the happiness of Brahman. With this, the Guru supplements the Akshi-Viḍyā, probably because it leads to the Lokas corresponding to it, viz., Sūrya loka. Then the Guru said: "Child, they (the Agnis) have spoken to you about lokas. I too will speak to you about them."

SAṬYAKĀMA-VIḌYĀ

FROM the Viḍyā of the disciple, we shall pass to the Viḍyā of his Guru, Saṭyakāma who in his turn had his own difficulties. This also occurs in the same Prapāthaka IV of *Chhānḍogya* previous to the former Khaṇdas, viz., IV. to IX. Saṭyakāma wanted to live in the house of his Guru as a Brahmachārin and so asked of his mother her goṭra. The mother Jābāla was unable to state it, on account of her not having inquired into the goṭra of one of the guests that had attended her husband's house and to whom he was born. Therefore passing under the name of Saṭyakāma Jābāla, the latter being the name of his mother, he went to Hāriḍrumaṭa to be his disciple. On the teacher asking him his goṭra, the young man made a clean confession that his mother had not known it. The Teacher said: "None but a Brāhmaṇa can say so. You have not departed from the truth. I shall invest you with the holy thread." After taking him as his disciple, the teacher selected four hundred lean and weakly cows and asked him to tend them. With his resolve of not returning to the house of his guru till the cows became a thousand, the disciple departed. When after many years the cows had multiplied into a thousand, a Bull asked him to take them back to the house of the teacher. Then it was, appreciating the true devotion and zeal of the disciple, the Ṛshabha (bull) and after it Agni, Sūrya and Maḍgu (Vāyu) taught him the four kalās or Pāḍas of Brahman. The Ṛshabha mentions the four Ḍiks or the quarters as the first kalā of Brahman, the meditation upon this quarter of Brahman as the Prakāśavān (shining) leading to the Prakāśaṭvam or renown of the devotee. Agni similarly descants upon the next pāḍa as Pṛṭhivī (Bhūḥ), Anṭariksha, Ḍyau and Samuḍra (ocean)—probably corresponding to Parjanya. The meditation is here as the Ananṭavān (endless). Sūrya says of the third Pāḍa as Agni, Sūrya, Chanḍra, and Viḍyut (lightning). It is to be meditated upon as the jyoṭishmān (effulgent). Maḍgu (vāyu) says of the fourth Pāḍa thus: Prāṇa eye, ear and Manas. It should be meditated upon as Āyaṭanavān, having them in the Āyaṭanam (or abode of body). After these instructions are over, the disciple goes to the house of the teacher where he was informed of the teachings given to his disciple as above mentioned and where the teacher sets his seal upon them as a Guru, since no teaching will fructify without the seal of the teacher.

The former teaching, viz., of Upkosala was from the standpoint of Agni merely. Here the feet of Brahman are described from the standpoint of the different directions (ḍiks), the lokas, the centres in them from which we have to rise from one loka to the other and the corresponding centres in the human body. Each meditation has its results. This knowledge merely supplements or explains that in the Ģāyaṭri-Viḍyā about the gates. All the worlds, Ḍevaṭās and centres of the body are only in the different Ḍiks of the One. Hence each direction is made a kalā or pāḍa of Him. Should one meditate upon the Ḍiks of the heart, he becomes Prakāśavān, i.e., one with the Prakāśa or light or renown everywhere. Should he meditate upon the Lokas, he rises above them to the eternal time and hence he is called Ananṭavān. Should he meditate upon the Ḍevaṭās of the world, he is gifted with the jyoṭis or spiritual light of them. Should he work in them centres of the body, he makes it an āyaṭanam or abode through which the spiritual influence is poured down. Hence he becomes an Āyaṭanavān. Thus He becomes or reaches the Saguṇa Brahman.

VAIS'VĀNARA-VIḌYĀ

In this connection we may deal with the Vais'vānara-Viḍyā too. Five gṛhasṭhas or householders met together and wanted to know something of Āṭmā and Brahman. They were great S'roṭriyas or knowers of the Veḍas. Their names were Prāchīnas'āla, Saṭyayajña, Inḍraḍyumna, Jana and Budila. Unable to come to any decision, they went to Uḍḍālaka Āruṇi who too was unable to solve their questions. Then all the five together with Uḍḍālaka went in a body to As'vapaṭi Kaikeya who had learned of the Vais'vānara Āṭmā. As'vapaṭi after finding that the wealth which he offered in sufficient quantity—his kingdom being one in which there were not thieves or other evil-minded persons—was not acceptable to them, they having come to him for the knowledge of Āṭmā, asked them to come on the morrow. When they came as fit disciples with the samiṭ (or fuel) in their hands, he asked them each a question as to the Āṭmā meditated upon by each. They said respectively the following: Ḍyau (Heaven), Sūrya, Vāyu, Ākās', Āpas and Pṛṭhivī. Thereupon the teacher said that each of them was but worshipping an aspect of Vais'vānara Āṭmā; its head is heaven or Suṭejas: its eye, Sūrya and Vis'varūpa; its breath,

Vāyu or Pṛṭhakvarṭmā (of various courses); its trunk or body is Ākās' (or Bahula); the Āpas is the moon, its fundament causing Rayī, the wealth; its feet, the Pṛṭhivī; his heart, the Veḍi (sacrificial platform); his hand, the sacrificial grass; his heart, the gārhapaṭya fire; his Manas, the Anvāhāryapachana fire and His face, Āhavanīya fire. Thus we find the Vais'vānara Āṭmā is said to be the Āṭmā pervading the three worlds: but in the description, the three fires are said to be in his universal body. Here the universal soul is described from the standpoint of Agni and the Upāsanā is conducted from the standpoint of Agni Vais'vānara only. Each of the householders that came for instruction is said to have obtained wealth or any other in the world according to that aspect of Vais'vānara which he took up for worship. Though this Agni has the three worlds in it, yet it is really the first Agni or Loka which consumes the food taken in. For it is in this connection the succeeding verses come which are related to Prāṇāgnihoṭra-Viḍyā and which have been described before. This viḍyā is dealt with in *Chhānḍogya*, V, xi. to xviii.

PAÑCHĀGNI-VIḌYĀ

THIS viḍyā is dealt with in *Chhānḍogya*, V, III. to X. and *Bṛhaḍāraṇyaka*, VI, II. as also in *Kaushīṭakī* briefly. Śveṭakeṭu, son of Uḍḍālaka Āruṇi, a Brāhmaṇa goes to the court of Pravāhaṇa Jaibali, a Kshaṭṭriya king who puts him certain questions which he is unable to answer. Returning to his father and finding him unable to answer them, he goes back to the king as a disciple and is explained the Viḍyā called the Pañchāgni-Viḍyā or Viḍyā of the five fires. As before explained, there are only three fires. How comes it now there are five fires? Besides the three fires of the three worlds, two more are given, viz., that in the man and that in the woman. The soul on its return from Svarga to be born again in a body has to pass through these five fires in order to get its fresh body. Naturally it is the fire that disintegrates the bodies as well as other things. How then can it be said to be the generator of forms? Fire has two functions, viz., to destroy as well as to create and preserve forms for the souls to tenant. The particles of Pṛṭhivī or earth are joined together through water and hence the required form is generated. But in order that the form may be kept intact, it is first exposed to the sun's heat and then burnt in the fire to be preserved for a long time. So also when the soul descends from the third world, it has to be provided with a body in each world. In each of these planes when it has to be provided with a body, an Agnihoṭra is performed for getting a body in each world. Take the Agnihoṭras performed in the physical plane. When oblations of rice, ghee, etc., are offered in the homakuṇḍa, Agni burns up into particles the oblations and carries them in a subtle condition to the Ḍevas invoked through the Manṭras. The reverse process also takes place in it. Take an illustration. In the sacrifice performed by Ḍas'araṭha, the Agni-Ḍevaṭā takes a physical shape and comes through the Agni with the Pāyasa or liquid food and after handing it over in a physical condition, disappears through the same channel. When a man's body becomes very hot or excited through some sudden cause, it begins to perspire. Similarly the same process takes place in this Viḍyā. When the soul, after all the enjoyments of Svarga are over, descends to the earth, it first takes up the mental body in the Rūpa plane of Svarga. The first Agnihoṭra therefore takes place in the third world; then the second body, in the astral world; then the third body in the physical plane. In the physical plane of ours, the soul attaches itself to rice and other things. The man eats them and then the fourth Homa takes place as Prāṇāgnihoṭra in the food digested by the man's body; when the seed of man is received into the womb of the woman, then the fifth Homa takes place and then is the physical body formed.

Here the instruction is given by the teacher to the disciple. The teacher begins by saying असौ वाव लोके "yonder in the loka". Afterwards the upward paths of the soul through the Devayāna and Pitṛyāna are described; the teaching winds up by saying in *Bṛhadāraṇyaka* that "those who thus know the (five Agnis), etc. . . . for them, there is no return to this world." In each of these five stages, there are not only the five Agnis but also the five oblations thereof in the shape of Water. The five Agnis are: (1) Svarloka (2) Bhuvar or Parjanya loka (3) Bhūr or Pṛthivī (4) man and (5) woman. The five water oblations are (1) S'raddhā (2) Somorājā (3) Varsha (rain) (4) Food and (5) Reṭas (seminal fluid). Thence the body is produced in the woman's womb. The first set of five is described as Agni and the second, as water. Out of the Agni in the three worlds as well as in man and woman, when the oblation is offered, the result in each stage is of a liquid nature. Hence all the five oblations are represented as water. We know that rain causes food; and the food which has to be taken into the system in a liquid condition is converted into Reṭas which also is liquid. Somorājā is Soma, the king of Piṭṛs. Piṭṛs are invoked in this world through the Ṭarpaṇa or water ceremony. Hence in the world in which the Piṭṛs are, they correspond to the water element and are (Ṭṛp) satisfied thereby. As regards S'raddhā or faith, it too is made to correspond to water in the heaven or third world. In the *Prasna-Upanishaḍ*, S'raḍḍhā is made to correspond to the soul, the essence of which is faith. In one of the Veḍas, it is stated that यज्ञ or Sacrifice is the husband and that S'raḍḍhā is the wife. The former is Agni and the latter is water. In the heavenly world, the Ḍevas offer in the Agnihoṭra S'raḍḍhā as the Āhuṭi or oblation, just as a priest having the Homakuṇḍa before him offers ghee and other articles to the fire in it.

What is the offshoot of it? Somorāja is born out of it, who is again offered in the lower world. Somorāja is explained by S'aṅkara as the form which the performers of sacrifice assume after death. Similarly what is born in one stage is offered in the next lower stage, in order to generate the still lower oblation and so on. S'ri S'aṅkara says the organs of the body in their relation to the soul are here the officiating priests of the Agnihoṭra. Considered in relation to the Ḍevas, they are Inḍra and other Ḍevas who are the officiating priests of the fire of Heaven, etc. They offer the fire sacrifice for the sake of the fruit; they perform the same sacrifice again. In this manner, the organs are called the Ḍevas. In this our present world also, any offering as ghee, milk, etc., thrown into the sacrificial fire and consumed by it enters, in its invisible subtile form together with the sacrificer, the Bhuvar world in the form of smoke and from the Bhuvar into the Suvar. There in the subtle waters, the effects of offerings—the part of the fire sacrifice—bearing the name of S'raḍḍhā, which create another body for the sacrificer in the world of the moon in the heavens are offered. Therefore the waters which are parts of the fire sacrifice and the cause that the sacrificer obtains another body in the world of the moon are called S'raddhā. This is the explanation for S'raddhā being called water. This is for going above. As above, so below.

In this Agnihotra there are in each stage the fire or Vedi, the fuel and the flame as well as those which issue out of the flame, viz., smoke, coals and sparks. All these six are put forth in these five stages. *Bṛhadāraṇyaka* has some differences in some points from *Chhāndogya* in their correspondence. In the heavenly world which is the Agnikuṇḍa, the fuel of Āditya, the sun, is placed whereby at first the smoke of his rays arises; and afterwards at the fire ignited, there arises the flame of the Day of the world. As regards the coal which arises after the flame subsides and the sparks which arise out of the flame, *Bṛhadāraṇyaka* puts them as the Ḍiks and Avāntara-Ḍiks, but *Chhāndogya* makes them the moon and the stars. These two sets are allotted by the above two Upanishads between the third and the first worlds. In the third world, the sun being the flame when the Agnihotra is finished, the coals should be naturally the moon and the sparks should be the stars. Similarly in the Parjanya or second world which is so called on account of Parjanya being the presider over rain or Āpas and which is the Vedi fire, the fuel is said to be, according to *Chhāndogya*, Vāyu and according to *Bṛhadāraṇyaka*, the Samvatsara or year and the clouds are the smoke and the lightning is the flame; the thunderbolt, the coals and the thunder-claps, the sparks. From this, it is clear that the rain we get is dependent upon the second world originally and condenses in this physical world; those that are mentioned above should be subtle only. Soma being here offered as an oblation, Varsham or rain comes out of it. In this physical world which is the Vedi fire, the fuel is given in the shape of Pṛthivī or years according to *Chhāndogya*. Naturally fire arises out of the earth as smoke from the fire; here earth being fire. The night is the flame, as the flame has its origin from the connection of fuel with fire, like the night from its connection with its fuel viz., earth; the darkness of the night being called the shadow of the earth. As regards coals and sparks, they have been already disposed of, in connection with the heavenly world. Here out of the oblation of rain comes the food or earth. In man and woman, the same process is described. In man, the Vedi fire, there is the fuel of the mouth where the flame of speech is generated. Prāṇa is the smoke; the eye the coals; and the ear, the sparks. The eye, viz., the coals can be lit up with the Kāma (passion) through sight. Similarly with regard to woman. After describing the downward process, the *Chhāndogya-Upanishad* afterwards expatiates upon the two paths through which we ascend to Saguṇa Brahman in the Devayāna Path.

SAMVARGA-VIḌYĀ

HAVING done with the western gate of the heart, we now come to the northern. Therein are Manas, Parjanya and Samāna. There is no separate Viḍyā attached to any of them. Therefore we shall have to pass to the upper gate where Vāyu and Ākās are. In regard to Vāyu, there is the Samvarga-Viḍyā. In the fourth Prapāthaka of *Chhānḍogya*, a king named Jānasruṭi Pauṭrāyaṇa is introduced in the first Khaṇḍa of the same. He was a person highly charitable in disposition and kept an open house to all, by feeding them at any time. Once while he was lying on his bed, two Hamsas passed in the sky over his palace; and one of them, finding that the Jyoṭis (effulgence) of the king was impeding their path, asked the other to fly away from it. To which the other replied by stating that the king could not be compared to Raikva with the one-wheeled car. The king who understood the language of birds asked the bards, who came to him next morning, to find out Raikva with the one-wheeled car. Finding him not, the king asked the bards to search for him in those places where Brahmajñānins are to be found, viz., in lonely places, river-sides, pools, mountains and groves. The great One was found sitting hard by a dilapidated wall with the one-wheeled car by his side and scratching the itches all over his body When the king was informed of it, he went to Raikva loaded with wealth and entreated him to initiate him into the Deity worshipped by him. The great One spurned him away from him. Thereupon the king increased the wealth and took his unmarried daughter too to be presented to him. Finding that there was now a real sacrifice on the part of the king, Raikva deigned to initiate him. From the cosmic standpoint, Vāyu is the Samvarga or ultimatum of all. Agni, Sūrya and Chandra merge into Vāyu only; so also Parjanya or Indra. From the individual standpoint, Prāṇa is the Samvarga of all. In sleep, Vāk, eye, ear and manas merge into Prāṇa only. Therefore the two Samvargas are Vāyu in the world and Prāṇa in the man. The word Samvarga is made to mean "absorbent" also, since it is the one into which all are merged from the lowest Pṛthivī to Agni inclusive. But Vāyu has in turn to become merged into Ākās' later on. In sleep or death, it is said by the Upanishads that the power of speech subsides into Manas and then both of them into Prāṇa.

In order to exemplify this, an episode is related in the same Upanishad to convey to us some truths about them. Two Brāhmanas named S'aunaka and Abhipratārin were being served at their meals, when a Brahmachārin asked for Bhikshā or alms-food. Nothing was given him by them, as they, according to S'aṅkara, wanted to try him. Thereupon the Brahmachārin said that in denying him food, they denied it to that one (Vāyu) which exists in all invisibly as the protector and the container of the four, Sūrya, Chanḍra, Agni and Āpas. Thereupon when the alms was given him, he remarked thus: "These five and five make ten and they are akṛṭa (complete number). Therefore anna (food) in the different quarters being ten is akṛṭa. It is Virāt, the consumer of food. Through it all, this becomes visible. Unto him who knoweth verily, unto him who knoweth this, all this world becomes visible and he becomes a great consumer of food."

From this, it is clear that in this viḍyā the individual Prāṇa has to be made to vibrate at the cosmic rate, viz., the Vāyu therein and that one who is a follower of this Viḍyā has not to deny food to any one. Rather this Viḍyā will be imparted to him only who is a person of great hospitality by giving food to others, as the Prāṇa in all is the one Vāyu which the disciple has to reach. That Vāyu in its highest state has in it the number ten which is a complete number. Through it, we can reach the Virāt of the Universe. The number ten is made to be the five Prāṇas and the five Upaprāṇas. It should be remembered that in the Ṭaṭṭvas Vāyu is said to be a Hexagon and Ākāś an egg. The Vāyu in the universe has in it a six-pointed star; in man, it is a five-pointed one. In the six-pointed star, there are 10 triangles—ten Agnis; there being 6 triangles externally and 4 triangles internally in the six-sided figure within it and the Agni Ṭaṭṭva having the figure of a triangle.

ĀKĀS'A-VIḌYĀ

In coming to Ākās', we find there are two places where the Ākās'a-Viḍyā is dealt with in the *Chhānḍogya-Upanishaḍ.* Three proficients in Uḍgīṭha met together for discoursing upon spiritual matters. They were named S'ilaka, Chaikiṭāyana and Pravāhaṇa. They began with the question of the gaṭi (asylum) of Sāma; one of them put the question and the other replied that Svara was the gaṭi: then the gaṭi of Svara was said to be Prāṇa: its gaṭi was Anna which was again traced to Āpas and Heaven. It was traced finally to the One. Then the question was asked of the Gaṭi of the Lokas or world. The reply was Ākāsa.

सर्वाणि ह वा इमानि भूतान्याकाशादेव समुत्पद्यन्त आकाशं प्रत्यस्तं यन्त्याकाशो ह्येवैभ्यो ज्यायानाकाशः परायणम् ॥ स एष परोवरीयानुद्गीथः स एषोऽनन्तः परोवरीयो हास्य भवति परोवरीयसो ह लोकाञ्जयति य एतदेवं विद्वान्परोवरीयांसमुद्गीथमुपास्ते ॥

—*Chhānḍogya-Upanishad*. I, ix. 1, 2.

"All these creations proceed from and end in the Ākās'. Ākās' is the senior of all these. It is the Parāyaṇa (great receptacle). It is the most excellent Uḍgīṭha. It is endless. He who knowing this adores the most excellent Uḍgīṭha conquers the most excellent Lokas. Such a learned person becomes most excellent." According to these passages, Ākās' is said to be the senior of all the Ṭaṭtvas and is the great receptacle, while Vāyu is said to be the consumer. It is also associated with Uḍgīṭha, since sound is the Ṭanmāṭra of Ākās'a. This Viḍyā occurs in I, IX. of *Chhānḍogya.*

In the same Upanishaḍ, Prapāthaka VIII, XIV. says thus:

आकाशो वै नाम नामरूपयोर्निर्वहिता ते यदन्तरा तद्ब्रह्म तदमृतꣳ स आत्मा प्रजापतेः सभां वेश्म प्रपद्ये . . . ॥१॥

"Verily that which is known as Ākās'a is made of Nāma-rūpa (name and form). That which is beyond the two (name and form) is Brahman. It is immortal. It is Āṭmā; I shall attain the Sabhām-Ves'ma (the audience hall) of Prajāpaṭi, etc." Here the Ākās'a is described as one with name and form and Brahman is beyond it. The Brahman here described is only the creator, Brahmā whose abode is given out.

GĀRGI-AKSHARA-VIḌYĀ

Janaka, the King of Videhas performed the yajña called Bahudakshiṇa (viz., of enormous gifts) in which many Brāhmaṇas were present. The King with a desire to know who amongst them was the Brahmajñānin caused to be tied 10 pāḍas of gold to each of the horns of a thousand cows and said that whoever amongst them was the best knower of Brahman might become their possessor. Ṛshi Yājñavalkya asked his disciple to drive them home, whereupon one after another in the assembly plied him with questions after questions. Gārgi Vāchaknavī put two questions to him, one about the Ākāśa and the other about Brahman. The first question was :

स होवाच यदूर्ध्वं गार्गि दिवो यदवाक् पृथिव्या यदन्तरा द्यावापृथिवी इमे यद्भूतं च भवच्च भविष्यच्चेत्याचक्षत आकाश एव तदोतं च प्रोतं चेति कस्मिन्नु खल्वाकाश ओतश्च प्रोतश्चेति ॥७॥ स होवाचैतद्वै तदक्षरं गार्गि . . . ॥८॥—*Bṛhaḍāraṇyaka*, III, viii.

"What is above the heavens, O Yājñavalkya, what is beneath the earth, what is between and what are these two, Heavens and earth, what is called the past, present and the future, upon what is all this woven, warpwise and woofwise? The reply is Ākāśa. Then the second question turned upon what the Ākāśa was woven warpwise and woofwise. The reply is Brahman, the indestructible One, O Gārgi." So that the Ākāśa is one in which are the vibrations, like the warp and woof of cloth. In two senses, the word Akāśa is used in the Upanishaḍs. The one is that it is that which yields अवकाशं or space for all the Taṭṭvas to fill it up. It is then Brahman, the Absolute Space. The other is that it is the Ākāśic Taṭṭva filling space. Then Ākāśa is defined as यत्सुषिरं तदाकाशं—that which is full of holes is Ākāśa. Then there are the warp and woof of ether in space. Then Ākāśa is said to be the cause of the three worlds; the three periods of time being in it.

Now that we have done with the five gates, we have to enter into the soul viz., jīvāṭmā itself which is said, in the Gāyaṭrī-Viḍyā, to be the Paramjyoṭis in the centre and beyond the five gates.

BHṚGU-VĀRUṆI-VIḌYĀ

First we shall enter into the Bhṛgu-Vāruṇi-Viḍyā, in order that we may know the different kośas or sheaths in which the soul is. In the *Taiṭṭirīya-Upanishaḍ* Bhṛgu, the son of Varuṇa is said to have approached his father for instructions in Brahman. The father leads him from one stage to another from the standpoint of Kośas, viz., Anna, Prāṇa, Manas, Vijñāna and Ānanḍa; and after stating the results of the meditation upon each of these kośas, he says: स यश्चायं पुरुषे ॥ यश्चासावादित्ये ॥ स एकः ॥ (*Brahmānanḍa-vallī*, 8). "He who is in the Purusha (of the eye) and who is in the sun is one and the same." Whoever thus knows after having transcended these kośas the soul which is in them as an assumer of any form at will and then realises the unity is the one who realises the supreme Brahman. Hence the idea of unity is essential for the attaining of Āṭmā.

ĀNANḌAMAYA-VIḌYĀ

In the same Upanishaḍ and in the previous or second Vallī which is called the *Brahmānanḍavallī*, we have the Ānanḍamaya-Viḍyā. In the fifth Anuvāka, we have the Ānanḍamaya-kos'a described which bliss is said to be above the kos'a of Vijñāna and to permeate it. Then this bliss is said to be of different degrees, beginning with that of a youth who is a sāḍhu well versed in the Veḍas and is firm, strong and of pure family. This bliss is said to increase one-hundredfold, as higher stages are reached, such as Manushya (men), Manushya-Ganḍharva, Ḍeva-Ganḍharva, Piṭṛs, Ājānaja-Ḍevas (born in heaven), Karma-Ḍevas, Ḍevas, Inḍra, Bṛhaspaṭi, Prajāpaṭi and Brahman. In this last stage, it is identified with the purusha in the sun and that in the eye. In all these stages, it is only the Veḍic or occult student free from desires that is able to enjoy all the degrees of bliss as stated above.

AṄGUSHṬHAMĀṬRA-VIḌYA

In the *Svetāsvatara-Upanishad*, the soul which is different from the S'arīras and the Kos'as is described as the Aṅgushṭhamāṭra. *Kaṭhopanishaḍ* also describes it in the same manner. In order to understand it fully, let me quote all the statements, of the same in the Upanishads. *Svetāsvatara* in v. 8 and 9 says:

अङ्गुष्ठमात्रो रवितुल्यरूपः संकल्पाहंकारसमन्वितो यः । बुद्धेर्गुणेनात्मगुणेन चैव आराग्रमात्रोऽप्यपरोऽपि दृष्टः ॥ वालाग्रशतभागस्य शतधा कल्पितस्य च । भागो जीवः स विज्ञेयः स चानन्त्याय कल्प्यते ॥

"The Aṅgushṭhamāṭra Purusha similar to the sun (in splendour) is endowed with Samkalpa and Ahamkāra. Associated with the guṇa of Buḍḍhi and the guṇa of Āṭmā (body), it is seen as another (different from Paramāṭmā) only, like the sharp point of a goad; the Jīva is to be thought of like the hundredth part of the point of a hair divided into a hundred parts. Yet it should be known that it is infinite."

Kaṭhopanishaḍ says thus in Vallī IV. 12 and 13:

अङ्गुष्ठमात्रः पुरुषो मध्य आत्मनि तिष्ठति । ईशानो भूतभव्यस्य न ततो विजुगुप्सत एतद्वै तत् ॥

The Aṅgushthamāṭra Purusha is located in the middle of the body, is the Īśāna (ruler) of the past and the future as well as the present. Hence one is not afraid of that. This is that.

अङ्गुष्ठमात्रः पुरुषो ज्योतिरिवाधूमकः । ईशानो भूतभव्यस्य स एवाद्य स उ श्व एतद्वै तत् ॥

"The Aṅgushthamāṭra Purusha which is like light without smoke and is the Īśāna (ruler) of the past and the future as well as the present is even to-day and will be verily to-morrow. This is that."

Again in the same Upanishaḍ, VI. 17, it says:

अङ्गुष्ठमात्रः पुरुषोऽन्तरात्मा सदा जनानां हृदये संनिविष्टः । तं स्वाच्छरीरात्प्रवृहेन्मुञ्जादिवेषीकां धैर्येण । तं विद्याच्छुक्रममृतं तं विद्याच्छुक्रममृतमिति ॥

"The Aṅgushthamāṭra Purusha which is the inner soul is always residing in the heart of men. Let one with courage separate it from his own body, like the stalk from the grass. Let him know it as pure and immortal: let him know it as pure and immortal."

As stated before, the soul is described with other similes; but the one thing that is to be borne in mind is that it is associated with this or that body, it is defined with its attributes. In its real nature, it is 'That' (Brahman); but in the state of the soul, it is different from the bodies and has Samkalpa and Ahamkāra, viz., I-ness that it is different from other souls. It should be remembered that the Jīva is in all Śarīras as well as in all Kośas. In the former the Jīva is named Vis'va, Ṭaijasa and Prājña as it is associated with the Sṭhūla, Sūkshma and Kāraṇa bodies. They are all associated with light in each world, each appearing as a speck of light. Only they are differentiated by the different vibrations of light. All of them have, in common, no form like that of the three bodies.

S'ĀṆDILYA-VIḌYĀ

In order to understand the nature or state of the soul, we may take up the Viḍyā called S'āṇdilya-Viḍyā. *Chhānḍogya-Upanishaḍ* devotes Aḍhyāya III, xiv. wholly to this Viḍyā. It says of the soul thus :

मनोमयः प्राणशरीरो भारूपः सत्यसंकल्प आकाशात्मा सर्वकर्मा सर्वकामः सर्वगन्धः सर्वरसः सर्वमिदमभ्यात्तोऽवाक्यनादरः ॥२॥ एष म आत्मान्तर्हृदयेऽणीयान्व्रीहेर्वा यवाद्वा सर्षपाद्वा श्यामाकाद्वा श्यामाकतण्डुलाद्वा एष म आत्मान्तर्हृदये ज्यायान्पृथिव्या ज्यायानन्तरिक्षाज्ज्यायान्दिवो ज्यायानेभ्यो लोकेभ्यः ॥३॥

"It is manomaya ; Prāṇa being its S'arīra and Bhā (effulgence) being its Rūpa. Saṭya is its Samkalpa ; Ākās'a is its Āṭmā (body). It is of all karma, of all Kāma, of all odour, of all Rasa, pervades all, neither speaks nor respects any. Smaller than a corn, or barley, or mustard or canary seed or the substance, it is within the heart. Such a soul is within the heart, as is greater than Bhūr, Bhuvar or Suvar world or all put together."

Bṛhaḍāraṇyaka in V, vi. is wholly devoted to this :

मनोमयोऽयं पुरुषो भाः सत्यस्तस्मिन्नन्तर्हृदये यथा व्रीहिर्वा यवो वा स एष सर्वस्येशानः सर्वस्याधिपतिः सर्वमिदं प्रशास्ति यदिदं किंच ॥१॥

"The Purusha which is manomaya has Bhā as its Saṭya, being within the heart like a grain of rice or barley. He is the Īs'āna of all (viz., the ruler of all). He overrules whatever exists in this universe." In the above two quotations, the soul, the Aṅgushthamāṭra is said to be in the heart and hence it is Prājña, the third. This has to be differentiated from the Jīva located in other centres being of the Jāgraṭ and other states. Here how is the meditation to be carried on? The soul should be meditated up as Bhā in the heart, it being in its inmost nature the Lord himself. Manomaya is interpreted by S'aṅkara to mean that which works in or through the Manas, as the soul is not Manas itself. In another place the soul is said to be Vijñānamaya. Janaka asked Yājñavalkya of the soul which was first stated by the latter to be the light of the sun, then the moon, then Agni and then speech: when all these disappear, in what state is the soul?

To which the reply is made thus: कतमआत्मेति योऽयं विज्ञानमयः प्राणेषु हृद्यन्तर्ज्योतिः पुरुषः स समानः सन्नुभौ लोकावनुसंचरति . . . . ॥७॥—*Bṛhadāraṇyaka*, IV, III.

What soul? "It is the Purusha of Jyoṭis, is Vijñānamaya and is in the heart within the Prāṇas; He being the same migrates to both worlds." Hence the soul may be meditated upon as the conscious light or the light with Manas, when the Manomaya Kos'a is to be reached: or with Vijñāna, when the Vijñānamaya Kos'a is to be reached. But then what do we mean by Prāṇa being its S'arīram, or body? The words are clear enough: but how is the idea to be realised in meditation? The physical body is preserved by the life of breath in this world: it is the breath, that makes the lungs to expand and contract. Similarly the growth of the soul in the higher condition is through the higher Prāṇa. Let us study how breath acts in this body. In inspiration, the breath makes the heart expand and in expiration the breath makes it contract. Hence expansion and contraction take place in the heart, which are called diastole and systole. Similarly the Prāṇa makes tho light of the soul expand and contract. Hence the soul appears as a dazzling light in contraction but diminishes in its lustre when it expands. When the Sāṇdilya-Vidyā is practised by one, he should meditate upon the soul as a speck of light like a corn or an atom expanding and contracting in the centre of the heart. But it is not a mere light but an intelligent light with Samkalpa and Ahamkāra as in the Aṅgushthamāṭra-Vidyā practice. As *Chhāndogya* puts it:

"It is Saṭya-Samkalpa pervading all like Ākās' and into which all things becomes merged." This is of Paramāṭman. But then what is the difference between Rūpa and S'arīra? Rūpa is a mere form or outline formed by the effulgence; whereas the bodily contour or configuration is imparted to it by Prāṇa.

ḌAHARA-VIḌYĀ

In this Viḍyā, the heart is described at greater length. *Chhāndogya*, VIII, I. says thus:

अथ यदिदमस्मिन्ब्रह्मपुरे दहरं पुण्डरीकं वेश्म दहरोऽस्मिन्नन्तराकाशस्तस्मिन्यदन्तस्तदन्वेष्टव्यं तद्वाव विजिज्ञासितव्यमिति ॥१॥ स ब्रूयाद्यावान्वा अयमाकाशस्तावानेषोऽन्तर्हृदय आकाश उभे अस्मिन् द्यावापृथिवी अन्तरेव समाहिते उभावग्निश्च वायुश्च सूर्याचन्द्रमसावुभौ विद्युन्नक्षत्राणि यच्चास्येहास्ति यच्च नास्ति सर्वं तदस्मिन्समाहितमिति ॥३॥

"Now within this Brahmapura (or city of Brahmā viz., human body), there is a small lotus chamber and within it is the Anṭar or inner Ākās'. That which is within the Anṭar Ākās' is worthy of search, that verily should be enquired after." "He (the disciple) would say: Verily as extensive as Ākās'a is, so is the Anṭar Ākās'. Both Suvar and Bhūr worlds (together with the Bhuvar) are within it. Both Agni and Vāyu, both the sun and the moon as also lightning and the stars and whatever else exist in this universe as well as what do not—all exist within this Anṭar Ākās'." A meditation on it is said to enable one to obtain all his desires; an enumeration of them being made in the Upanishaḍ. In the second S'loka, third

Khaṇḍa of the same Prapāthaka of the Upanishad, it says:

यथापि हिरण्यनिधिं निहितमक्षेत्रज्ञा उपर्युपरि संचरन्तो न विन्देयुरेवमेवेमाः सर्वाः प्रजा अहरहर्गच्छन्त्य एतं ब्रह्मलोकं न विन्दन्त्यनृतेन हि प्रत्यूढाः ॥

"As those who are ignorant of (mineral) beds might pass repeatedly over an undiscovered mine of gold and find it not, so do mankind daily retire into the Antar Ākās' (in Sushupṭi) and yet being misled by Anṛta (Māyā), they find not this Brahmaloka." In this Vidyā, the all-pervading nature of this one is described or laid stress upon. Hence the heart is called Hṛdayam, or the formless which means, this is the heart or place where the Aliṅga is. Even in the Bālāki-Vidyā as also in *Bṛhadāraṇyaka*, the soul is in sleep with Brahman alone. In this meditation, the three worlds in the heart as well as all the creations in them have to be meditated upon.

BĀLĀKI-VIḌYĀ

In the *Kaushīṭakī-Upanishad*, the fourth Aḍhyāya is devoted to this Viḍyā alone. A person named Gārgya, the proud son of Bālāki who was renowned as a reader of the Veḍas wandered about for Brahmajñāna till he came to Ajāṭas'aṭru, the King of the Kās'īs, when he applied to him for instruction about Brahman. Having been asked his own understanding of the question, the disciple stated first Brahman to be the Purusha of the sun; then that of the moon: then of lightning, thunder bolt, Ākās', Vāyu, Agni, Āpas, Mirror, Echo, sound, the sleeping state, the body, the right eye and the left eye. The teacher after stating at each step that each of the above Purushas served but a lower purpose took the disciple to a man who was asleep. After awaking him from his sleep, the master told the disciple that the soul called Prājña was absorbed in the Prāṇa of the heart that works on the Nāḍīs issuing from the one Nāḍī of the heart, Purīṭaṭī and that all the organs together with then presiding ḍevaṭās that were in that condition came out like sparks from flames, illuminating the lower purushas (Ṭaijasa and Vis'va) and the lower bodies down to the nails and hairs of the skin. Then (in the last sloka) he winds up thus :

स यावद्ध वा इन्द्र एतमात्मानं न विजज्ञौ तावदेनमसुरा अभिबभूवुः स यदा विजज्ञावथ हत्वासुरान्विजित्य सर्वेषां भूतानां श्रैष्ठ्यं स्वाराज्यमाधिपत्यं पर्यैति तथो एवैवं विद्वान्सर्वेषां भूतानां श्रैष्ठ्यं स्वाराज्यमाधिपत्यं पर्येति य एवं वेद य एवं वेद ॥

"As long as Indra knew not this soul, so long as the Asuras overcame him. When he knew it, then having conquered and slain the Asuras, he attained the pre-eminence of all devas and all beings : he attained sovereignty and empire. Thus too is it with him who hath this knowledge, having destroyed all sins—and he attaineth the pre-eminence of all beings and sovereignty and empire—who knoweth thus—who knoweth thus." This occurs also in *Bṛhadāraṇyaka* II, 1.

USHASṬA-KAHOLA-VIḌYĀ

As related in the *Bṛhaḍāraṇyaka*, III, iv. and v. in the sacrifice performed by Janaka where Ṛshi Yājñavalkya takes the cows as a Brahmajñānin, two of the querists were Ushasṭa Chākrāyaṇa and Kahola Kaushīṭaka. The previous questioners had queried the Ṛshi with questions about the bondage of Grahas and Aṭigrahas with which the soul is bound. Then Ushasṭa puts the question to the Ṛshi as to यत्साक्षादपरोक्षाद्ब्रह्म य आत्मा सर्वान्तरस्तं or Brahman which is the real and direct one and as to the Āṭmā which is within all. The second reply after a further question is यः प्राणेन प्राणिति स त आत्मा सर्वान्तरः "It is thy soul which breathes through the (five) Prāṇas that is in all." Then again when the questioner wanted a further explanation like the description of a cow or horse, the reply came that it could not be given, as one could not perceive the perceiver of all perception. Then comes the next chapter where Kahola puts the same question for further information as to the means by which the soul which seems to be different from Brahman can be cognised as one. 'Renunciation of all,' is the reply. Having known the Āṭmā, the Brāhmaṇas rise above the desires for sons, wealth and worlds and lead the lives of wandering mendicants. The desire for sons is also the desire for wealth; when the desire for wealth arises, there is obtained a twofold wealth. The physical wealth enables one without knowledge to do rites which will take him to Pitṛloka; but the higher wealth, viz., Knowledge leads one to Ḍevaloka. Hence the desire for wealth leads to the higher worlds of Pitṛs and Ḍevas. Therefore after getting knowledge, he should arm himself with Bala, literally strength or indomitable will. After both these are obtained, he should be able to practise at will Mauna and Amauna, when to be silent and when not. Such a one is Brāhmaṇa, no matter in what work he is engaged. He is then above work. In these two meditations, the soul has to be meditated upon as one with Brahman.

UḌḌĀLAKA-ĀRUṆI-VIḌYĀ

In the same connection, there is another Vidyā recorded where Uḍḍālaka is one of the questioners. He said to Yājñavalkya thus : "In order to study the science of Yajña, others and myself were pupils of Paṭañchala Kāpya. His wife was possessed by a Gandharva named Kabanḍha, son of Aṭharvaṇa who put us the two questions of the Sūṭra or thread binding all objects and the Anṭaryāmin or latent one in all. Please explain to us the Sūṭra and the Anṭaryāmin." The Ṛshi's reply is that Vāyu is the Sūṭra or thread which binds all worlds and things. It is Vāyu in the world or Prāṇa in man ; when it is relaxed, death takes place in the body. Then as regards the Anṭaryāmin, he gives a long list of the many things of the world in which He (the Āṭmā) is latent and winds up with the reply :

नान्योऽतोऽस्ति द्रष्टा नान्योऽतोऽस्ति श्रोता नान्योऽतोऽस्ति मन्ता नान्योऽतोऽस्ति विज्ञातैष त आत्मान्तर्याम्यमृतोऽतोऽन्यदार्तम्

"There is none that sees but He ; there is none that thinks but He ; there is none that intuits but He. He is thy soul, the Anṭaryāmin, the immortal ; whatever is different from Him is perishable."—*Bṛhaḍāraṇyaka-Upanishaḍ*, III, VII. 23.

MAIṬREYĪ-VIḌYĀ

To the same category, the Viḍyā under consideration belongs. In the *Bṛhaḍāraṇyaka-Upanishaḍ* it occurs, in II, iv. and IV, v. With a little difference in details, the one is reproduction of the other. Ṛshi Yājña-valkya had two wives, Maiṭreyī and Kāṭyāyanī. Of them, the former was devoted to spirituality and the latter, to household duties. Ere the sage retired from his household life, he wanted to distribute his property among his two wives. Kāṭyāyanī was of course content with the prospect of what she could get thereby; but the other addressed her husband with the question as to whether the wealth to be obtained could secure to her immortality. The sage stating that renunciation of all was the only means for it proceeded to initiate her into the Higher Āṭmā with all the explanations possible through those famous passages that are generally quoted. The concluding passages run thus:

न वा अरे सर्वस्य कामाय सर्वं प्रियं भवत्यात्मनस्तु कामाय सर्वं प्रियं भवत्यात्मा वा अरे द्रष्टव्यः श्रोतव्यो मन्तव्यो निदिध्यासितव्यो मैत्रेय्यात्मनो वा अरे दर्शनेन श्रवणेन मत्या विज्ञानेनेदꣳ सर्वं विदितम् ॥

"Behold not for the sake of all (the universe) all (the universe,) is dear; but for the sake of Āṭmā, all (the universe) is dear. Behold, the Āṭmā is verily to be seen, heard, thought and intuited. Behold, O Maiṭreyī, by seeing, hearing, thinking and intuiting the Self (Āṭmā), all this (universe) is known." II, IV. 5. The teacher in order to lead her from the dual to the non-dual says at last: एवैतेभ्यो भूतेभ्यः समुत्थाय तान्येवाऽनु विनश्यति न प्रेत्य संज्ञास्तीति—"Arising with these elements, he (the individual soul or the division of a particular soul, as S'aṅkara puts it) is destroyed when they are destroyed. After leaving the body, there is no Saṃjñā (viz., the highest stage of individualised knowledge)." II, IV. 12. Then he says:

यत्र हि द्वैतमिव भवति तदितर इतरं . . पश्यति . . . . यत्र वा अस्य सर्वमात्मैवाभूत्तत्केन कं जिघ्रेत्तत्केन कं पश्येत्तत्केन . . केन विजानीयात्—II, IV. 14.

"For where there is duality as it were, there sees another, another thing . . . .; but how does one to whom all has become Āṭmā alone smell anything? how see anything? . . . .; behold how should he intuit the knower."—As S'aṅkara puts it, "It is only when cause and effect are differentiated, there is the concept of duality: all are one in the state where cause and effect are blended into one, (rather) are one only."

PARAM-PURUSHA-VIḌYĀ

THEN we shall deal with the Param-Purusha-Viḍyā. It occurs in the third Vallī of *Kathopanishaḍ* in the reply of Yama to Nachiketas. This should be distinguished from another Viḍyā called Purusha-Viḍyā. The opening Manṭra deals with two Āṭmās entering the guha of the heart.

ऋतं पिबन्तौ सुकृतस्य लोके गुहां प्रविष्टौ परमे परार्धे । छायातपौ ब्रह्मविदो वदन्ति पञ्चाग्नयो ये च त्रिणाचिकेताः ॥—*Kathopanishaḍ*, I, III.

"The two drinking the due reward from their works in this world entered both the cave, the highest place of the supreme. Brahmaviṭs call them shadow and sunlight; thus also the performers of Pañchāgni and the sacrificers of the three Nāchiketāgni. How is the meditation to be carried on? As stated further on:

आत्मानं रथिनं विद्धि शरीरं रथमेव तु । बुद्धिं तु सारथिं विद्धि मनः प्रग्रहमेव च ॥३॥ इन्द्रियाणि हयानाहुर्विषयांस्तेषु गोचरान् । आत्मेन्द्रियमनोयुक्तं भोक्तेत्याहुर्मनीषिणः ॥४॥

इन्द्रियेभ्यः परा ह्यर्था अर्थेभ्यश्च परं मनः । मनसस्तु परा बुद्धिर्बुद्धेरात्मा महान्परः ॥१०॥ महतः परमव्यक्तमव्यक्तात्पुरुषः परः । पुरुषान्न परं किंचित्सा काष्ठा सा परा गतिः ॥११॥

"Know the Āṭmā to be the rider, the body as the chariot; know Buḍḍhi as the charioteer and Manas as the reins. They say the senses are the horses, their objects are the roads. The wise say thus: The enjoyer is the soul associated with body, sense and mind.—Higher indeed than the Indriyas (senses) are their objects; higher than their objects is Manas; higher than Manas is Buḍḍhi: and higher than Buḍḍhi is the great Āṭmā. Higher than the great one is Avyakṭa; higher than Avyakṭa is the Purusha; higher than the Purusha is naught; this is the last limit and the highest goal." The means for attaining the Param-Purusha is

यच्छेद्वाङ्मनसी प्राज्ञस्तद्यच्छेज्ज्ञान आत्मनि । ज्ञानमात्मनि महति नियच्छेत्तद्यच्छेच्छान्त आत्मनि ॥१३॥

Let the wise subdue his speech by Manas; the Manas by the *Jñāna-Āṭmā*; the *Jñāna-Āṭmā* by Mahaṭ, (the great-soul); subdue this also in the Śānṭa-(peaceful) Āṭmā.

It should be through the Guru.

उत्तिष्ठत जाग्रत प्राप्य वरान्निबोधत । क्षुरस्य धारा निशिता दुरत्यया दुर्गं पथस्तत्कवयो वदन्ति ॥१४॥

"Arise, awake, attain the great (Teacher) and be Illumined. The wise say that the path to him is as difficult to tread as the sharp edge of a razor."

From these, it is clear that there are two Āṭmās, the higher and the lower. The lower or embodied soul is the rider in the chariot who has to be the master of the situation by subduing one after another, viz., Speech,

Manas, Jñāna-Āṭmā and Mahaṭ, till at last he reaches the S'ānṭa-Āṭmā or the Āṭmā of Peace which has to be reached through the Jīvanmukṭa of a Guru.

But in the above quotation, the higher Āṭmā is also represented as drinking the fruits of its actions as well as the lower. Here the two Āṭmās are made to be one. In order to state that the Paramāṭmā is not, other quotations about the two birds seated on a tree will be pertinent. Here Paramāṭmā being associated with Jīvaṭmā seems to eat the fruits, but is not really eating. *Muṇḍaka*, III, I. 1, 2, and *Sveṭāsvaṭara*, IV. 6, 7, are to the same effect. They may be quoted :

द्वा सुपर्णा सयुजा सखाया समानं वृक्षं परिषस्वजाते । तयोरन्यः पिप्पलं स्वाद्वत्त्यनश्नन्न्योऽभिचाकशीति ॥ समाने वृक्षे पुरुषो निमग्नोऽनीशया शोचति मुह्यमानः । जुष्टं यदा पश्यत्यन्यमीशमस्य महिमानमिति वीतशोकः ॥

"Two birds (Paramāṭmā and Jīvāṭmā) ever united and equal companions dwell on one and the same tree (of body): one of them (viz., Jīvāṭmā) enjoys the sweet fruits of the fig tree: the other (Paramāṭmā) looks round as a witness—Dwelling on the same tree, the deluded soul (viz., Jīvāṭmā) immersed (in the world) is grieved by the want of power ; but when it sees the other, the worshipped ruler as different (from all worldly relations) and his glory, then its grief vanishes."

In this meditation, the fruits of actions have to be given up to reach the Paramāṭmā.

AKSHARĀKSHARA OR AKSHARA-PARĀ

Two aspects of Brahman, the Akshara are dealt with from the standpoint of Vidyā or knowledge. *Muṇḍaka*, I, 1. 4 says thus :

द्वे विद्ये वेदितव्ये इति ह स्म यद्ब्रह्मविदो वदन्ति परा चैवापरा च ॥

Two Vidyās should be known, the higher and the lower, thus tell us the Brahmavits.

तत्रापरा ऋग्वेदो यजुर्वेदः सामवेदोऽथर्ववेदः शिक्षा कल्पो व्याकरणं निरुक्तं छन्दो ज्योतिषमिति ॥ अथ परा यया तदक्षरमधिगम्यते ॥५॥

The lower comprehends the Ṛg, the Yajur, the Sāma and the Atharva Vedas., S'ikshā, Kalpa, Vyākaraṇa, Nirukta, Chhandas and Jyotisha; the higher is the Vidyā by which the indestructible (Brahman) is realised.

यः सर्वज्ञः सर्वविद्यस्य ज्ञानमयं तपः । तस्मादेतद्ब्रह्म नाम रूपमन्नं च जायते ॥९॥

"From Him who is Sarvajña, Sarvavit, Jñānamaya and Tapas is generated Brahmā (Hiraṇyagarbha) with Nāma (name) and Rūpa (form) and annam (food). Hence it is that Hiraṇyagarbha or Brahmā with Nāma and Rūpa presides over the world itself." Here food is that substance which enables the form to act.

SAḌ-VIḌYĀ

In *Chhāndogya*, VI, ii. 1 and 2, we have S'veṭakeṭu being enlightened by his father, Uḍḍālaka regarding this Saḍ-Viḍyā. It runs thus:

सदेव सोम्येदमग्र आसीदेकमेवाद्वितीयं तद्धैक आहुरसदेवेदमग्र आसीदेकमेवाद्वितीयं तस्मादसतः सज्जायत ॥ कुतस्तु खलु सोम्यैवं स्यादिति होवाच कथमसतः सज्जायेतेति सत्त्वेव सोम्येदमग्र आसीदेकमेवाद्वितीयम् ॥

"At first, O Son, this was mere Saṭ, one only without a second. Thereof verily others say: At first this was Asaṭ, one alone without a second; from that Asaṭ proceeds Saṭ".

He continued: "But of a truth, O Son, how can this be? How can Saṭ proceed from Asaṭ? At first O Son, this was only Saṭ, one only without a second."

We all know that this is quite in agreement with the statement of modern science. A thing should create another thing; and nothing should generate nothing only. In the *Bhagavaḍ-Gīṭā*, ii. 16, S'ri Kṛshṇa also says the same thing, नासतो विद्यते भावो नाभावो विद्यते सतः । 'There is no Bhāva (existence) to Asaṭ: There is no Abhāva (non-existence) to Saṭ.' The commentator in this connection states that the statement here embodied that there was "only Saṭ, one alone without a second", out of which all else arose, was meant to rebut the statements made by two sets of doctrinists in India, viz., Vaiśeshikas and Bauḍḍhas. The former held that the origin of the universe lay in a number of causes, viz., Ḍravya, Guṇa and Karma. Here Uḍḍālaka tells us that there is only one cause, without even a second, of this universe viz., Saṭ. Again some Bauḍḍhas and others hold that the universe which is Saṭ or something, arises out of Nothing. Thus there is only one cause of all these visibles and invisibles and that cause is not Asaṭ, but Saṭ.

In this connection, another passage in the same Upanishaḍ may be taken into consideration which passage seems to militate with thus. In *Chhānḍogya*, III, XIX. the first verse runs thus:

आदित्यो ब्रह्मेत्यादेशस्तस्योपव्याख्यानमसदेवेदमग्र आसीत्तत्सदासीत्

"Āḍiṭya (the sun) is described as Brahman. Its description: Verily at first all this was Asaṭ; that Asaṭ became Saṭ." How is it that the author here states that all this was Asaṭ at first and that from Asaṭ came Saṭ. Here the commentator says that the word Asaṭ stands for the Avyakṭa or unmanifested state devoid of name and form. From it, the universe of name and form arose—that original state being one of darkness which is but a higher form of light.

BHŪMA-VIḌYĀ

THIS Viḍyā also is to be found in the seventh Aḍhyāya of the same Upanishaḍ. It contains the initiation into this Viḍyā of Nāraḍa by Sanaṭkumāra. After Nāraḍa had related the many books he had studied, the teacher said that that study was but in name and led the disciple from one stage to another; from name to Vāk; from Vāk to Manas; from Manas to Samkalpa; from Samkalpa to Chiṭṭa; from Chiṭṭa to Ḍhyāna; from Ḍhyāna to Vijñāna; from Vijñāna to Bala (strength); from Bala to Annam (food); from Annam to Āpas; from Āpas to Ṭejas; from Ṭejas to Ākās'a; from Ākās'a to Smara (memory); from Smara to Āsā (desire); then to Prāṇa. Then when the teacher said that Prāṇa was all these and that he who sees, thinks and intuits the relationship and nature of the Prāṇas became an Aṭivāḍī. Nāraḍa then became silent. Thereupon the teacher enunciated one after another the qualifications of the disciple for initiation, viz., Saṭya, Vijñāna-maṭi (the zeal to know), S'raḍḍhā (faith), Nishkala and Kṛṭi (S'ānṭi), which qualifications Nāraḍa complied with at each stage. Then the teacher said: Sukham (happiness) therefore is worthy of inquiry. The disciple said:

"That happiness, O Lord, is sought by me." Then in Section XXIV. the teacher said of the Bhūma-Viḍyā thus:

यत्र नान्यत्पश्यति नान्यच्छृणोति नान्यद्विजानाति स भूमाऽथ यत्रान्यत्पश्यत्यन्यच्छृणोत्यन्यद्विजानाति तदल्पं यो वै भूमा तदमृतमथ यदल्पं तन्मर्त्यं . . . ॥१॥

"Where one cannot see another, where one cannot hear another, where one cannot intuit another, that is the Bhūmā (great); where one can see another, where one can hear another, where one can intuit another, that is the Alpam (small). Verily that which is Bhūmā is immortal, that which is Alpam is mortal." Thus is the Bhūma-Viḍyā related by Sanaṭkumāra to Nāraḍa to reach that state where the "I" or the soul is stated to be everywhere. In the closing verse of this chapter is made a statement that he who realises thus confronts neither death nor disease and becomes manyfold. In the numbers given, the highest is 1,000 which means that the soul can manifest itself in 1,000 forms, as Śrī Kṛshṇa was seen by Nāraḍa in the many Gopins' houses. In the centre of the head called Sahasrāra, it has 1,000 petals or spokes through which such manifestations arise.

PARYAṄKA-VIḌYĀ

In the first chapter of *Kaushīṭaki*, it is related that Chiṭra Gārgyāyaṇi wanted to perform a sacrifice, for which he sent for Uḍḍālaka as priest who sent his son S'veṭakeṭu to officiate for him. When the son went, Chiṭra put some questions to S'veṭakeṭu, similar to those put to him by the King Pravāhaṇa Jaibali. The son unable to answer them returned to the father. Both of them being ignorant resorted to Chiṭra as pupils in quest of knowledge, when Chiṭra initiated them in the Viḍyā called the Paryaṅka or couch of Hiraṇyagarbha or Brahmā. It is said there that the moon is the door of Svarga and makes the soul—that rejects it, i. e., has got over desires—to pass beyond it through the Ḍevayāna path to the Brahmā world; but in the case of the soul that rejects it not, it makes it return for rebirth in the physical world. In this Viḍyā, the soul is made to pass beyond the moon. First it goes to the world of Viḍyuṭ (or lightning); then the Guru comes across his path and puts the question: Who art thou? In the reply, the S'ishya traces all his path, till he says: 'I am time. I am dependent on time'; the reply not being satisfactory, when further pressed with the question

कोऽसि—Who art thou ?, the reply is त्वमसि, 'I am thyself'; then it is that the disciple is allowed to proceed onward. Then the worlds of Agni, Vāyu, Varuṇa, Inḍra, Prajāpaṭi or (Virāt) and lastly Brahmā are reached. In the last world, the world of Hiraṇyagarbha, there is Brahmā seated on his couch called Paryaṅka. Hence this Viḍyā is called by that name.

Before Brahmā is reached, we have to describe all the stages through which the pilgrim has to go. Ere he reaches Brahmaloka, the first thing he has to cross is the lake called *Īra* from *Ari*, the enemies of desire, etc. But the *Chhānḍogya* describes there two lakes *Īra* and *ṇya*; hence *Araṇya*, forest; then the Muhūrṭā Yeshtihā (or the Sacrifice destroying moments); then the Virajā river on the banks of which is situated the tree called Ilya; then the City of Brahmā called Sālajya Samsṭhāna. In it is the palace called the Aparājiṭa Āyaṭanam or impregnable palace. Then the door-keepers, Inḍra and Prajāpaṭi have to be confronted. Then Brahmā's Hall, called विभु प्रमितं is reached, where there is a throne called Vichakshaṇa in the centre of which is the couch of immeasurable radiance called Paryaṅka. As soon as the pilgrim reaches the Virajā River, Brahmā asks the attendants of his to go to and receive him with all the respects due to him. The Apsaras, the nymphs of heaven, are deputed for this work, who go with fruits, perfumes, garlands, garments and powdered aromatics and adorn him with the adornments of Brahmā. When he goes to Brahmā seated on his couch with the pillows, he mounts the couch with one foot at first. Brahmā asks him कोऽसि—Who art thou? He should reply thus:

ऋतुरस्म्यार्तवोऽस्म्याकाशाद्योनेः संभूतो भार्यायै रेतः संवत्सरस्य तेजोभूतस्य भूतस्यात्मभूतस्य त्वमात्मासि यस्त्वमसि सोऽहमस्मीति तमाह कोऽहमस्मीति सत्यमिति ब्रूयात्किं तद्यत्सत्यमिति यदन्यद्देवेभ्यश्च प्राणेभ्यश्च तत्सदथ यद्देवाश्च प्राणाश्च तद्यं तदेतया वाचाभिव्याह्रियते सत्यमित्ये-तावदिदं सर्वमिदं सर्वमसि . . . ॥

—*Kaushītakibrāhmaṇa-Upanishad*, I. 6.

"I am Ṛṭū (time), I am what is in time. I am born from the womb of Ākāsa; the seed of wife; from the Samvaṭsara (year); the Ṭejas of Bhūṭas (elements); the Āṭmā of all and the five elements. Thou art Āṭmā; what art thou, that am I." Brahmā says to him: "Who am I". Let him answer "Thou art Saṭya." (Brahmā asks:) "What is Saṭya? What is other than the Ḍevas (senses) and Prāṇas, that is Saṭ; what is the Ḍevas and Prāṇas, that is that ṭya; all this is called by the word Saṭṭya (truth). Such is all this universe. All this art thou." Herein is another division of Saṭṭya.

Then this conversation is continued thus. Brahmā asks him, How dost thou obtain the male names? By Prāṇa. How neuter names? By Manas. How female names? By Vāk. Then one after another of the organs are questioned, till all that is to be known and desired are related to their source, viz., Prajñā. Thus is the Hiraṇyagarbha Loka reached where all the extended power of चितिः (victory) and व्याप्ति (power) await him who reaches it. As *Veḍānṭa-Sūṭras* put it in Aḍhyāya IV, iv. 17, he who reaches it gets even the power of creating, preserving and destroying the worlds. Only he will not be allowed to exercise it, as there will occur a conflict between the rightful authority and the one reaching it.

Though the description given here of Brahmaloka, is of a concrete form, it will be found in the Upanishaḍ that when the disciple reaches the lokas he has to journey through his Manas alone. All the concrete things have to be made abstract. First about the lake Āra. This lake according to S'aṅkara is one that stops the entrance to the world of Brahmā, its depth being equal to a hundred oceans and its dark waters ever flowing in it, viz., tremendous waves, etc. It is called Āra, as it is composed of the Arí-shad-vargas or the six enemies of Rāga, Ḍvesha, Kāma, Kroḍha, Maḍa and Māṭsarya. In the *Chhānḍogya-Upanishaḍ*, it is stated that Brahmacharya or celibacy alone will enable one to overcome the two lakes of Āra and Nya, which two terms when coupled together are Āraṇya or forest where celibacy was practised by the Vānaprasṭhas. The lake can best be imagined as space with the undulatory force of subtle matter ever rolling fiercely or vibrating at a very rapid rate, like the waves of the ocean. Only those who have conquered love and hate and other pairs can cross this lake mentally. For it should be remembered that all the journeyings here have to be done through Manas—nay—Prajñā at a later stage of the journey.

Next comes the Muhūrṭā Yeshtihā. It is translated as the sacrifice—destroying—moments. Those that produce Rāga, Ḍvesha, etc., destroy the sacrifice which enables one to attain Brahmā. Now that the disciple has crossed Āra and Nya lakes of Rāga, Ḍvesha, etc., those periods of time that produce them fly naturally from him. Similarly there is the Virajā River and the Ilya tree on the other side of the river in which is the Brahmā-city. The crossing of this Virajā or ageless river enables him to never grow old. Then he is able to live to the age of Brahmā—he who had been subject to birth and death again and again in the lower worlds. Formerly the desires of love and hate were seething like the waves of lakes having a limit to them and then subsiding; but there comes the river which is continuously flowing without any limit to its period or age. Hence one having had a snāna or dip inṭo it is rejuvenated and made free from the limitations of the age and lives even to Brahmā's age, since even Brahmā has his limit of age. In it, all his good and bad karmas are shaken off, the good ones going to his dear kindred; his enemies getting the evil ones, of course committed in past lives. It is the gulf of Lethe which is between the Brahmā world and the lower worlds. One has to cross it with full memory. When this ageless river is crossed, he sees the Ilya or Ilpa tree from which the odour of Brahmā reaches him. This is the first organ of sense, viz., that of smelling, crossed in the Brahmaloka. Then comes the Sālajya City which affects the mouth through its flavour. This is the second organ of sense, viz., tasting crossed. Then comes the organ of seeing in Brahmā's palace, wherefrom the Ṭejas reaches him. Then come the door-keepers, Inḍra and Prajāpaṭi who represent, according to Śaṅkara, Vāyu and Ākāśa and who fly from him. Ahaṃkāra, the sixth, is represented by Vibhu, the hall of Brahmā, whence the glory, viz., the feeling of pride "I am Brahmā" reaches him. Then comes Mahaṭ which is represented by the throne, Vichakshaṇa. This is Prajñā from the standpoint of consciousness. The Text says: सा प्रज्ञा प्रज्ञया हि विपश्यति—"It is Prajñā: through Prajñā, he sees it all." Brahmā sits on this throne, since Mahaṭ is the totality of matter over which he presides. In other words, this one totality of matter is the real matter with which Brahmā is clothed.

Now about His throne. As the Text says: स आगच्छति विचक्षणामासान्दींबृहद्रथन्तरे सामनी पूर्वौ पादौ घ्यैत नौधसे चापरौ पादौ वैरूपवैराजे शाकररैवते तिरश्ची—He comes to his throne Vichakshaṇa: The Sāmas Bṛhaḍ and Raṭhanṭara are its eastern feet: The Sāmas Ḍhyaiṭa (or Śyaiṭa according to other texts) and Nauḍhasa, its western feet: the Sāmas Vairūpa and Vairāja, Śākvara and Raivaṭa forming its horizontal sides." These Sāmas are said to be the names of the Hymns in the Sāmaveḍa. Probably it is in these sounds of the Sāmaveḍa lie the maximum and minimum of sound impulses of Mahaṭ to create forms. All these sounds are latent in the matter of Mahaṭ with which Brahmā is clad.

But there is another thing to connect Brahmā with his garment. Just as in man the Jīva is connected with the matter of the Nādīs through Prāṇa, so there is the one intermediate Prāṇa between Brahmā and his throne of Mahaṭic matter. On his throne is the Paryaṅka or couch of unmeasured ojas or aura. स प्राण: "This is Prāṇa." As the Text itself says in I. 5. In other words, this is the Hamsa on which Brahmā bestrides in the lower or Rūpa worlds. As Hamsa is the vehicle of the Jīvas in the lower worlds, so the couch of Prāṇa is made to be over the throne; Mahaṭ representing or standing for the collective Jīvas. It is in the state of Ahamkāra, the Jīvas became separated. But in Mahaṭ they are one. With regard to his couch, तस्य भूतं च भविष्यच्च पूर्वौ पादौ श्रीश्चेराचापरौ बृहद्रथन्तरे अनूच्ये भद्रयज्ञायज्ञीये शीर्षण्यमृचश्च सामानि च प्राचीनातानं यजूंषि तिरश्चीनानि सोमांशव उपस्तरणमुद्गीथ उपश्रीः श्रीरुपबर्हणं—"The two feet of the couch are S'rī (the lower prosperity) and the earth (or Prakṛṭi). The two other feet are the past and the future, while all the hymns of the different Veḍas are posted at the bars and cornices of the couch. Time and matter of the worlds with their Pravṛṭṭi S'rī are posted at the lower end of the couch; while the Nivṛṭṭi S'rī is at the upper end of the couch serving as the pillow of Brahmā. The Upa S'rī of the Udgīṭha Brahmā is as the cushion for Brahmā to dally with. The Nivṛṭṭi S'rī at the upper end is the Priyā or wife of Brahmā who is, as stated in another place, the cause of

Manas, viz., Mānasī; and the Pravṛṭṭi S'rī is her Praṭirūpa or reflection which is the cause of the Chakshus or Chākshsushī who weaves the world like flowers; the Upa S'ri of Uḍgīṭha is represented by the 700 Apsaras who are the mothers of all, the undecaying and the streams that roll on to the knowledge of Brahmā." Five hundred of them go to receive the pilgrim with fruits: one hundred with garlands and one hundred with the Chūrṇam (fragrant powder) in their hands. Hence the cause of Manas standing for eye and sound standing for ear and Vāk are there. Brahmā rests on the moon as his bed, since it is that which has come from the past universe and is the seed of the new universe. The sun is not here found, as the sun's jurisdiction stops with the three worlds. The sounds of all the Veḍas that have proceeded from the one sound, viz., the Uḍgīṭha above are at the corner, etc., of the couch.

From the foregoing it is clear that even in the Brahmaloka there are two aspects, the Avyakṭa and the Vyakṭa. It is the world in which the *aṇu* or atom and the Mahaṭ or the great (viz., the Extremes) meet. Hence we find two stages in which there seems to be repetition. In the Vyakṭa stage or the Mahaṭ stage, we find the Mahābhūṭas and Ahamkāra and Mahaṭ represented by the Ilya tree, Sālajya, Aparājiṭa palace, Inḍra and Prajāpaṭi (standing for the five elements) as well as the hall Vibhu and the throne

Vichakshaṇa that stand for Ahaṁkāra and Mahaṭ. These are manifested externally. But going right into the centre, we find Brahmā seated on Prāṇa, his couch. In order to create the universe, Hiraṇyagarbha breathes it forth through Prāṇa, his vehicle. It is stated that the universe is exhaled by Brahmā at the time of Kalpa and inhaled by him at Pralaya. Prāṇa is the Fohatic power through which Brahmā does the work. In *Liṅga-Purāṇa*, it is stated to be the Ananṭa, the eternal time through which the universe is enacted or breathed forth. Hence time is made the two feet of the couch. This Prāṇa is under the control of Brahmā and hence it is his couch. This couch has all the materials latent in it for Brahmā to create the world or to weave the worlds like flowers, as the Upanishaḍ puts it, In other words Prāṇa has the two powers, viz., the outgoing or ingoing—the lower part of the couch and the upper part. In the lower, the Śrī and Prakṛṭi, viz., Purusha and Prakṛṭi are there to create with finite time at the other end of the feet; while above there are moon, the latent one having Ahaṁkāra and Mahaṭ, the cause of mind, the cause of the eye and the Uḍgīṭha, the cause of sound. All the causes of the elements, etc., are there which are taken by the lower sets to manifest in the Brahmaloka itself as patent things; for these again are manifested in still more concrete shapes in the lower lokas or worlds. Therefore this Viḍyā is called Paryaṅka or couch, as in it all the universe is latent. Thus therefore the Brahmā world may be described in a diagram thus from the concrete standpoint:

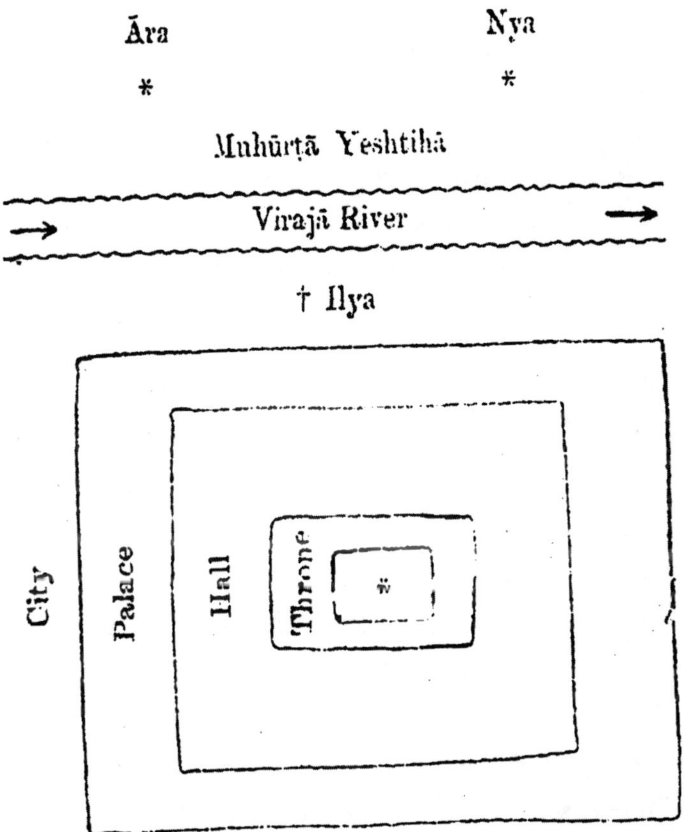

(The Star in the centre represents the Paryaṅka.)

JYOṬISHĀM JYOṬIRVIḌYĀ

This is the Viḍyā communicated by Ṛshi Yājñavalkya to Rājarshi Janaka. The fourth Aḍhyāya of *Bṛhaḍāraṇyaka* commences with the teachings and goes over four Brāhmaṇas or chapters. In the second Brāhmaṇa Ṛshi Yājñavalkya introduces three kinds of souls, Vis'va, Ṭaijasa and Prājña as having their respective centres in the body in the three Avasthās.

इन्धो ह वै नामैष योऽयं दक्षिणेऽक्षन्पुरुषस्तं वा एतमिन्धꣳ सन्तमिन्द्र इत्याचक्षते परोक्षेणैव परोक्षप्रिया इव हि देवाः प्रत्यक्षद्विषः ॥२॥ अथैतद्वामेऽक्षणि पुरुषरूपमेषास्य पत्नी विराट् तयोरेष सꣳस्तावो य एषोऽन्तर्हृदय आकाशोऽथैनयोरेतदन्नं य एषोऽन्तर्हृदये लोहितपिण्डोऽथैनयोरेतत्प्रावरणं यदेतदन्तर्हृदये जालकमिवाथैनयोरेषा सृतिः संचरणी यैषा हृदयादूर्ध्वा नाड्युच्चरति यथा केशः सहस्रधा भिन्न एवमस्यैता हिता नाम नाड्योऽन्तर्हृदये प्रतिष्ठिता भवन्त्येव ताभिर्वा एतदास्रवदास्रवति तस्मादेष प्रविविक्ताहारतर इवैव भवत्यस्माच्छारीरादात्मनः ॥३॥

"Inḍha is verily the name of the Purusha who dwells in the right eye. Him whose true name is Inḍha, they call Inḍra by an indirect name. For the gods like indirect names and dislike to be named directly. Again that which in the shape of a Purusha dwells in the left eye is his wife, the Virāt. The union of them is (in) the ether within the heart; again their food is the lohiṭa-piṇda (red-mass) within the heart; again their place of retreat is like the net-work (of Nādis) in the heart. Again the path to be travelled on (from Jāgraṭ to Svapna) is the Nādī which rises up from the heart. Like the hair a thousand times divided, thus are the Nādīs called the Hiṭā, which are located in the heart. Proceeding by these Nādis, that food proceeds. There is as it were food more subtle than that. From this soul of the body (is nourished the higher)."

Then in the next Brāhmaṇa he proceeds to state in what world the Jīva is.

तस्य वा एतस्य पुरुषस्य द्वे एव स्थाने भवत इदं च परलोकस्थानं च मध्ये तृतीयः स्वप्नस्थानं तस्मिन्मध्ये स्थाने तिष्ठन्नेते उभे स्थाने पश्यतीदं च परलोकस्थानं च . . . . . स्वेन भासा स्वेन ज्योतिषा प्रस्वपित्यत्रायं पुरुषः स्वयंज्योतिर्भवति ॥९॥

"There are even two places of this Purusha, this place and the place of the next world; the place of dream which is between them is the third. Abiding in this middle place, man sees both places . . . . . Himself creating a building (dream body) through the force of his own Bhāsa and Jyoṭis, he sleeps: then this Purusha becomes Svayam-Jyoṭis (self-light)." The seat of this Purusha is described as being in the heart thus:

कतमआत्मेति योऽयं विज्ञानमयः प्राणेषु हृद्यन्तर्ज्योतिः . . . ॥७॥

"What is the soul (Āṭmā)? That Āṭmā which is Vijñānamaya, which is within the heart and within the Prāṇas and which is the Purusha of Jyotis." Then the next Brāhmaṇa leads the Purusha to the highest. This Purusha which is the pure light of Brahman has to return to this world through kāmas or desires but does not, when it is devoid of desires. "Being even a Brahman he obtains Brahman." Then it says in the fourth Brāhmaṇa thus:

यस्मादर्वाक्संवत्सरोऽहोभिः परिवर्तते ।
तद्देवा ज्योतिषां ज्योतिरायुर्होपासतेऽमृतम् ॥१६॥
यस्मिन्पञ्च पञ्चजना आकाशश्च प्रतिष्ठितः ।
तमेव मन्य आत्मानं विद्वान्ब्रह्मामृतोऽमृतम् ॥१७॥

"O Ḍevas, make an Upāsanā of this Jyoṭishām Jyoṭiḥ (or the Light of lights) as the immortal life after whom the year with its days is rolling again and again. I, the wise, the immortal comprehend as the immortal Brahman, the soul upon which the five kinds of beings and Ākās' are founded." Here is the Viḍyā of Jyoṭishām Jyoṭiḥ described. It ends thus in IV, iv. 22:

स वा एष महानज आत्मा योऽयं विज्ञानमयः प्राणेषु य एषोऽन्तर्हृदय आकाशस्तस्मिञ्छेते सर्वस्य वशी सर्वस्येशानः सर्वस्याधिपतिः . . . ॥

"This great unborn Āṭmā is the Āṭmā which abides as Vijñānamaya, within the Prāṇas, in the Ākās' of the heart; in it, it sleeps: it is the subduer of all; the Lord of all; the sovereign Lord of all". This is a meditation from the standpoint of consciousness. It is from Vijñānamaya-kos'a.

ĪSA-VIḌYĀ

In the *Isāvāsya-Upanishaḍ*, the opening lines commence thus:

> ॐ ईशावास्यमिदꣳ सर्वं यत्किंच जगत्यां जगत् ।
> तेन त्यक्तेन भुञ्जीथा मा गृधः कस्य स्विद्धनम् ॥१॥
> *　　*　　*　　*　　*
> यस्मिन्सर्वाणि भूतान्यात्मैवाभूद्विजानतः ।
> तत्र को मोहः कः शोक एकत्वमनुपश्यतः ॥७॥

"All this, whatever changes in the changing world must be God-vestured. Be happy through renouncing it; covet not (aught; for) whose is wealth?—Who knoweth all things as Āṭmā, for him what grief existeth, what delusion when once he gazeth on the Oneness." Thus are we led to the Oneness from the universe. For even the Hiraṇya-garbha described in the Paryaṅka-Viḍyā is subject to delusion, being the seed of all the universe. Therefore is it called S'abala or Saguṇa Brahman as opposed to the Nirguṇa. We all know the famous passage of *Kenopanishaḍ*, II. 3. यस्यामतं तस्य मतं मतं यस्य न वेद सः । where it is said that he who thinks he knows Brahman, (the Nirguṇa) does not know him, as all knowledge implies a duality The Nirguṇa being the non-dual one, is only a subject of realization.

SRĪMAN-NYĀSA-VIḌYĀ

Though the above subject is included under the heading of Viḍyās by some, others do not consider it so. It occurs in the Ṭaiṭṭirīya Nārāyaṇam and does not rightly come under the Upanishaḍs. The key-note of it is Nyāsa or renunciation to Brahman. As the *Kaivalya-Upanishaḍ* puts it in I. 2, न कर्मणा न प्रजया धनेन त्यागेनैके अमृतत्वमानशुः ॥ "Persons attain Salvation not through Karma, progeny or wealth but through renunciation alone." This renunciation is called Samnyāsa Yoga in another place.

Now we have done with the Viḍyās. Of the 32 Viḍyās, those of Prāṇa and Praṭarḍana have been treated of as one in this work; while Prāṇāgnihoṭra which is related to Vaisvānara-Viḍyā has been dealt with separately, as it is an important subject by itself. To the 32 Viḍyās, two Viḍyās which Srī Sankara mentions in his Commentary on the *Veḍānṭa-Sūṭras*, viz., Uḍgīṭha- and Purusha-Viḍyās are added in this book.

From the foregoing, it is clear that all these Viḍyās lead one from the heart, viz., Kārana Sarīra to Saguṇa Brahman. Naturally our Veḍānṭins whose eye is on that One above Māyā will not fall short of the

Absolute and hence look down upon all the meditations which lead to Saguṇa Brahman and hence to the ultimate Māyā only. Some even go to the extent of saying that Punarjanma or rebirth will await one who goes to the Saguṇa. But such is not the opinion of S'rī S'aṅkara. In the very last Sūtra of *Vedānta-Sūtras* अनावृत्तिशब्दात्, अनावृत्तिशब्दात्, he clearly says thus in his commentary :

सम्यग्दर्शनविध्वस्ततमसां तु नित्यसिद्धनिर्वाणपरायणानां सिद्धैवानावृत्तिः । तदाश्रयणेनैव हि सगुणशरणानामप्यनावृत्तिः सिद्धिरिति

"It is a settled matter that those who through Samyag-Ḍars'ana (perfect vision) have dispelled all mental darkness and are devoted to the eternally perfect Nirvāṇa do not return; and as those also who rely on the knowledge of Saguṇa Brahman in the end have recourse to that (Nirvāṇa), it follows that they also do not return."

From the above passages there is no doubt that those who meditate upon Saguṇa Brahman reach the Nirguṇa in the end. When the Saguṇa reaches the Nirguṇa, they also reach It. But then there is the next question whether those who wish to reach the Nirguṇa have to pass through the Saguṇa. If they have to pass through the Saguṇa in reaching the ultimate goal, then it cannot be argued that the meditation upon the Saguṇa is unnecessary for them too.

AFTERWORD

We have now come to the end of a most difficult and abstruse subject. The Vidyās are, as said above, different kinds of meditation. They are meant for advanced souls who scale from the third world to the fourth and thence to the higher worlds, till they reach the highest. But in taking up the different kinds of meditation, each soul has to adopt one which is suited to its growth and nature in the scheme of evolution. These souls may be roughly divided into two classes—those that want to reach the goal alone and those that want to work in the world too. The former are the Jīvanmukṭas that wish to raise themselves to the Videhamukṭi condition of the highest by throwing off all bodies. The latter are the Jīvanmukṭas who want to work in the world and are called Āḍhikārika-Purushas. Naturally the former take up Āṭmā for meditation; the latter, though they may take up Āṭmā, meditate upon that which is their specialty. In the latter case, in order to fulfil the office which they take up, they resort to certain meditation adapted to their office. Without taking into our consideration the highest offices of Brahmā, Vishṇu and Śiva, there are others which the souls have to occupy. To begin with, there are the five elements over which preside the five Ḍeva souls. If in the future a soul has to occupy the place of fire, it has now to meditate solely upon fire as the aspect of Āṭmā and make a specialty of it. Similarly there are the other offices of the sun, moon, Ḍhruva, earth and others over which reside other souls. Coming down to this earth of ours which is presided over by Sanaṭkumāra, we find there are some who live with him with meditation alone as food. Then there are the two chief positions of the Ruler and the priest; then there are the other positions of presiding over a portion of earth, etc. At different periods in this earth, one has to incarnate as a great Bhakṭa; another to set an example of Karma; another to give an impetus to Jñāna. For which purpose each soul has to incarnate at different periods to do that work. Such an one should therefore have his special work and meditation suited to his work. Only it should be remembered that such souls as are Āḍhikārika-Purushas have to live in the bodies of the globe they live in to give impetus to the souls therein. Hence it is that different kinds of Viḍyās are given in the Upanishaḍs. It were better this subject had been handled by some occultist able to see the higher states and relate his experiences. It is perhaps to expedite the advent of such a person this book has been written.

INDEX